Intro to Bitcoin

Intro to Bitcoin

Hope for a better world

Erin E. Malone

Featuring contributions and charts

by Sage Sokol-Lanting

Copyright © 2024 Erin E. Malone

All rights reserved.

ISBN: 9798322916277

No portion of this book may be reproduced in any form without written permission from the publisher or author.

The content in this book is for informational purposes only, you should not construe any such information or other material as legal, tax, investment, financial, or other advice.

Table of Contents

Acknowledgments 1

Foreword 3

Introduction
What is Bitcoin? 5

Glossary of Terms 8

Part 1

Bitcoin: A New Hope 15

Chapter 1
The Lightning Network: 16
    FUD #1: Bitcoin is slow
    Money at the Speed of Light
    Micropayments

Chapter 2
Bitcoin Mining and Energy 22
    FUD #2: Bitcoin uses too much energy/using energy is bad.
    Stranded Energy
    Oil Wells
    Landfills
    Energy Infrastructure
    Grids
    Low-Grade Heat
    Energy Use
    FUD #3: The 51% Attack

Chapter 3
Financial Freedom and Human Rights 45
    Banking the Unbanked
    Women's Rights

   Refugees
   Activism
   Remittance Payments
   Asset Seizure

Part 2

Fiat: The Corruption Strikes Back 51

Chapter 4
Money 101 52
   Fiat Currency
   Money is Time
   The Money Spigot
   Debt
   Gold
   Some Problems with Gold
   Properties of Bitcoin
   Security
   FUD #4 Bitcoin has no intrinsic value
   Unit of Account and Medium of Exchange
   FUD #5: Isn't there a better coin?
   FUD #6: Only criminals use Bitcoin
   FUD #7: The government will ban Bitcoin
   Nation State Adoption

Part 3

The Future: The Return of Sound Money 87

Chapter 5 88
Lessons
   Saving and Personal Accountability
   Time Preference

Chapter 6 92
Hope for the Future
   A Deflationary World

A Peaceful World
A Prosperous World
Game Theory

Final Thoughts *99*

Endnotes *100*

Acknowledgments

Thank you to Sage for keeping me sane and reminding me to eat and sleep throughout this entire process. Thanks for allowing me to bounce ideas off you and for discouraging me from writing about advanced Lightning Node running strategies, UTXO management, the Byzantine General's Problem, and all the technical topics that would have made people run from this book.

Thank you to all my friends and family who read early drafts and gave invaluable feedback.

Thank you to John for all "that" help.

And thank you to all the amazing Bitcoin educators who first sent me down the rabbit hole.

FOREWORD

I wrote this book for my mom to understand Bitcoin. I wrote this for all my friends whose eyes glaze over the moment Bitcoin is mentioned. I wrote this for everyone who has said, "But what if the government bans it?" or "Isn't it just a Ponzi scheme?" or "Bitcoin is just too complicated for me." I wrote this for all of them.

I looked far and wide for a good introductory book to hand out to people, but it didn't exist. So, I took it upon myself to write one. My goal was to produce a concise, straightforward guide free of technical jargon—a book anyone could easily understand and enjoy.

This book explores a wide range of topics, including the Lightning Network and payment technologies, how Bitcoin mining interacts with worldwide energy systems, and Bitcoin's role in promoting human rights. It also examines how our monetary systems have evolved, addresses common myths about Bitcoin, and explores the future possibilities that come with adopting Bitcoin. I hope this book serves as a helpful and approachable introduction as you begin your Bitcoin journey.

Introduction
What is Bitcoin?

Bitcoin is money.

Bitcoin is the first perfectly engineered money with all the attributes that make money appealing without any of the flaws. Today, millions of users worldwide store their wealth in bitcoin and use the Bitcoin network to send and receive peer-to-peer payments, without going through a third party such as a bank, a government, or a company.

Bitcoin is math.

Bitcoin is the culmination of over fifty years of advancements in cryptography. Many have tried to create a digital currency, but Bitcoin was the first one to ingeniously combine all the optimal attributes of money while addressing all the systemic issues of any money that came before it. Essentially, it solved the math and logic problems of the previous failures. The Bitcoin codebase, called Bitcoin Core, was created by an anonymous founder named Satoshi Nakamoto. In the midst of the great financial crisis of 2008, Satoshi released a white paper—a concise nine-page document that outlined the mathematics, coding, and functional elements of Bitcoin. This code has been running reliably for over 15 years on millions of computers worldwide.

Bitcoin is a system of rules, not rulers.

Once set in motion on January 3, 2009, with the Genesis block (the first block of Bitcoin), a block has been found approximately every 10 minutes since. Every new block contains all the new transactions submitted by users moving bitcoin. This is how all the transaction data gets stored on the blockchain forever, which is saved automatically on all the computers worldwide running the Bitcoin Core software. It's a transparent system where anyone can audit every transaction since the first block. Block discovery is done by a process called Bitcoin mining, which is essentially guessing really big numbers for a reward. We'll dive into Bitcoin mining in Chapter 2.

Bitcoin is the first money free from government influence.
No government, organization, company, or person controls Bitcoin. This is one of the features that separates bitcoin from any other currency today.

Bitcoin is a network.

Since the Genesis block, Bitcoin has grown exponentially. The network now consists of millions of users sending value across the world. There are hundreds of thousands of users running Bitcoin Core software on their computers. Each computer, or "node," runs a copy of Bitcoin Core, which includes both the rule set that governs the network and the ledger that records every bitcoin transaction over time. This ledger, known as the blockchain, is a public record of all blocks that have ever been mined. It ensures transparent ownership by documenting to whom each bitcoin belongs. These nodes serve as validators to ensure all transactions comply with Bitcoin's rules. Any illegal transaction that does not follow the rules gets rejected.

Anyone can opt into this system. It is an open network, allowing anyone with an internet-connected device to download a wallet, send or receive bitcoin, run a node, or mine bitcoin without needing permission. A prime example of such an open network is the internet itself.

Glossary of Terms

1. **ASICs:** Application-Specific Integrated Circuits (ASICs) are computers designed for a single, specific purpose.
2. **Base Chain/Main Chain:** The main blockchain of Bitcoin where all standard transactions are recorded. The base chain maintains core properties such as the ledger of transactions, new bitcoin issuance through mining, and decentralized consensus. This layer is fundamental to Bitcoin's operation, ensuring security and immutability of the data. It is distinct from additional layers like the Lightning Network, which enhance functionality or scalability.
3. **'B' Bitcoin:** Uppercase Bitcoin refers to Bitcoin the network.
4. **'b' bitcoin:** Lowercase bitcoin refers to bitcoin the asset.
5. **Bitcoin Core:** The official software that runs the Bitcoin protocol.
6. **Block:** A collection of transactions recorded during a specific time period, permanently documented on the blockchain through mining. Each block contains a list of recent transactions and references the previous block, with successful miners earning rewards in bitcoin from the block subsidy and transaction fees.
7. **Block Subsidy:** The amount of bitcoin a miner receives for successfully mining a block. This does not include bitcoin received from transaction fees.
8. **Blockchain/Timechain:** Also referred to as the "timechain" by Satoshi, the blockchain contains a record of every Bitcoin block mined since its inception. Each block documents all transactions for that moment and is found, timestamped, and added to the chain approximately every 10 minutes.
9. **Cantillon Effect:** An economic theory that suggests money creation disproportionately benefits those who are closest to the source of production.
10. **Closed Network:** A controlled network restricted to authorized participants only.

11. **Coin Issuance:** A total of 21 million bitcoin will be awarded to miners as block subsidies from 2009 until 2140. As of now, over 19 million bitcoin have been mined. The last full coin will take around 40 years to mine.
12. **Cold Wallet:** A highly secure method for storing private keys offline, making it resistant to hacking. The overall security also depends on the specific setup and handling practices. A cold wallet is typically on a secure hardware device. Transactions can be signed from this device with one's private key.
13. **Consensus:** The process used by network nodes to agree on the validity of transactions, ensuring each node's copy of the distributed ledger is the same. This system is crucial for maintaining the integrity and security of the blockchain.
14. **Crypto:** An abbreviated form of the word 'cryptocurrency,' it is now used as slang to refer to all other coins that are not bitcoin.
15. **Debt Spiral:** A negative feedback loop of falling deeper into debt by borrowing more money to pay off previous debts, akin to using a Mastercard to pay off a Visa.
16. **Deflation:** A decrease in the general price level of goods and services over time, leading to an increase in the purchasing power of money.
17. **Difficulty Adjustment:** A mechanism built into the Bitcoin protocol to regulate the rate at which new blocks are added to the blockchain, ensuring one new block approximately every 10 minutes. The difficulty of mining Bitcoin is adjusted every 2016 blocks, or roughly every two weeks, based on the total computing power of the network. If miners collectively contribute more computing power, the difficulty increases to maintain the 10-minute block time. If computing power decreases, the difficulty decreases to maintain the same block time. This adjustment helps to ensure the stability and security of the Bitcoin network.

18. **Exahash:** A unit of measure equal to one quintillion hashes per second, used to quantify the computational power in Bitcoin mining.
19. **The Federal Reserve:** The central banking system of the United States, established in 1913. The 'Fed' sets monetary policy, regulates banks, maintains financial stability, and provides financial services to depository institutions, the U.S. government, and foreign official institutions.
20. **Flaring:** The process of burning excess natural gas, primarily methane, which is released during oil extraction or from sources such as landfills. This practice converts methane, a potent greenhouse gas, into CO_2, which has a lower global warming potential. However, flaring operations are not completely efficient; on average, they release about 9% of the methane unburned into the atmosphere.
21. **Fiat:** An authoritative decree. Fiat refers to government-issued currency that is not backed by a physical commodity, such as gold or silver. Instead, fiat's value comes primarily from the trust and faith people have in the government that issues it. The term "fiat" means "by authoritative decree" and is Latin for "let it be done," signifying the currency has value because the government decrees it to be legal tender. Some examples of fiat currencies today include the dollar, peso, lira, pound, euro, yuan, and yen.
22. **FUD:** stands for fear, uncertainty, and doubt. The term is often used to describe spreading false or misleading information to influence perception.
23. **Game Theory:** The study of strategic decision-making, considering the interdependent actions of multiple decision-makers. In the context of Bitcoin, it analyzes the strategic interactions among network participants, especially miners, exploring how they can maximize rewards under the network's rules. It also considers the game theory of adoption, where individuals are incentivized to join and support the network, enhancing its overall value and security. This study includes

analyzing miners' incentives, likely actions, competitive environment, and the incentives for new users to adopt Bitcoin.

24. **Genesis Block:** The very first block of Bitcoin mined on January 3, 2009, by Satoshi Nakamoto. Within the raw data, he included the message "The Times 03/Jan/2009 Chancellor on brink of second bailout for banks," which was the newspaper headline of *The Times*, a London based newspaper, on that day.

25. **Grid:** (electrical) A vast network of power stations, transmission lines, and distribution systems that delivers electricity from producers to consumers. Your home is most likely connected to this grid, which is how you receive electricity.

26. **The Halving:** Approximately every four years, or 210,000 blocks, the block subsidy gets cut in half. The block subsidy began with 50 bitcoin per block, then went to 25 four years later and so on. I'm writing this definition on the day of the 4th halving, April 19, 2024, when the block subsidy changed from 6.25 to 3.125 bitcoin. The process will continue until all 21 million bitcoin are mined around the year 2140. There will be 32 total halvings.

27. **Hashrate:** A measure of the computing power per second used to mine and process transactions on a proof-of-work blockchain, like Bitcoin.

28. **Hot Wallet:** A wallet connected to the internet. These may facilitate easier transactions but poses a higher risk compared to cold wallets (offline wallets) due to potential online security vulnerabilities.

29. **Hyperinflation:** An extremely high and typically accelerating rate of inflation, often exceeding 50% per month, leading to a rapid decrease in the currency's purchasing power.

30. **Inflation:** The rate at which the general level of prices for goods and services rises, eroding purchasing power and reflecting a decrease in the value of a currency over time.

31. **The Lightning Network:** A "second layer" payment protocol that operates on top of Bitcoin. It enables split-second transactions and allows Bitcoin to scale by handling transactions off the main blockchain.
32. **Methane:** A powerful greenhouse gas that traps heat at a rate 84 times greater than CO_2 over the first 20 years, and 28 times more heat than CO_2 over the following 100 years as it breaks down. Oil wells, landfills, and agriculture emit methane as a byproduct of their operations.
33. **Micro Grid:** Small-scale power networks that operate independently from the main grid to distribute electricity to localized areas.
34. **Micropayments:** Very small payments. On the Lightning Network, these payments happen as sats or millisats, which are worth a fraction of a penny today. Micropayments are great for tipping on social media or streaming small payments to content creators.
35. **Millisat:** 1/1000th of a satoshi. Since there are 100,000,000 satoshis in one bitcoin, there are 100 billion millisats in one bitcoin.
36. **Miner:** Refers either to the ASIC (Application-Specific Integrated Circuit) computer used for mining bitcoin, or to the individual who owns and operates such a device.
37. **Mining Pool:** A collective group of Bitcoin miners who combine their hashrate to increase the probability of mining a block, affording each a more consistent share of the rewards than mining alone.
38. **Money:** A shared belief system where the value and utility are recognized and accepted collectively by society. Money is not valuable in itself but becomes valuable because people agree to use it as a store of value, a medium of exchange, and a unit of account. This consensus allows money to facilitate transactions and coordinate economic activity effectively.

39. **Node:** A node is a computer connected to the Bitcoin network that runs Bitcoin Core to validate transactions and blocks, maintaining the integrity and security of the blockchain.
40. **Open Network:** A network that is accessible to anyone without any restrictive criteria for participation. It allows for the free flow of information or transactions and is not controlled by a single entity or group, promoting inclusivity and collaboration among its users.
41. **Order 6102:** An executive order signed by U.S. President Franklin D. Roosevelt on April 5, 1933. This required U.S. citizens to deliver all gold coin, gold bullion, and gold certificates held by them to the Federal Reserve, in exchange for $20.67 per troy ounce. This action allowed the government to inflate the currency. Satoshi Nakamoto listed his birthday as April 5, and every difficulty adjustment is 2016 blocks, or Order 6102 in reverse.
42. **Petrodollar:** The practice of selling crude oil in U.S. dollars, a standard established in the 1970s following agreements between the U.S. government and oil-producing countries. This system reinforces the U.S. dollar's dominance in the global economy, requiring oil-importing countries to hold large reserves of dollars to facilitate trade.
43. **Proof of Work:** A decentralized consensus mechanism that requires network members to expend hashrate in solving an encrypted very large number, ensuring network security. Contributing hashrate requires an expenditure of energy and incurs real-world costs.
44. **Public/Private Key:** A cryptographic tool in Bitcoin to facilitate transaction security. The public key is shared openly and used to receive funds, while the private key is kept secret and used to sign transactions, proving ownership of one's bitcoin. Storing a private key on a device connected to the internet creates security vulnerabilities.

45. **Remittance Payments:** Transfers of money by foreign workers to individuals in their home country, often a vital source of income for families in developing regions.
46. **Satoshis or "Sats":** A smaller unit of bitcoin. One bitcoin is divisible into 100 million satoshis.
47. **Seed Words:** A sequence of 12 or 24 words generated by a Bitcoin wallet, which provides the information needed to recover Bitcoin funds in the event of wallet loss or damage. Storing these words on an internet-connected device poses security risks.
48. **Stranded Energy:** Energy produced in remote areas far from electrical grids and human populations, which cannot be consumed locally. This energy remains unused because transmitting it to populated areas is not cost-effective or is technically challenging.
49. **Unbanked:** Individuals who lack access to traditional banking services, such as bank accounts or credit. Reasons for this include geographical barriers, insufficient documentation, or economic exclusion.
50. **Unit Bias:** A cognitive bias in which individuals prefer owning whole units rather than fractional parts. They assess an item's value based on its price per unit rather than its overall market value, frequently disregarding critical factors such as total supply, market capitalization, and fundamental value. For instance, while some may hesitate to buy a full bitcoin priced at $70,000, they might opt to purchase 1,000 lesser-known coins at a penny each, perceiving greater value in acquiring more units.

Part 1
Bitcoin: A New Hope

I believe Bitcoin is the biggest and most significant innovation since the internet. Part 1 is everything that captivates me about Bitcoin, all the aspects I find world-changing and cool, and everything I think you should know up front.

Chapter 1

The Lightning Network

"What the internet did for communication, Bitcoin and the Lightning Network is doing for money."

-Jack Mallers, CEO of Strike

Our current global monetary system is a slow, clunky antiquated dinosaur, full of obstacles and roadblocks, lacking the speed and accessibility essential for today's national and global financial landscape. Is Bitcoin the solution? Bitcoin is not a company. No one controls Bitcoin. It operates as an open-source system maintained by millions of users worldwide, without any central authority controlling it. No other coin, token, or currency shares these unique characteristics.

In the past, Bitcoin has faced criticisms for its relatively slow transaction processing time, which takes an average of 10 minutes. This is by design.

FUD (Fear, Uncertainty, and Doubt) #1:
Bitcoin is slow. It takes an average of 10 minutes to send a transaction.

The solution to this "slow" processing time is the Lightning Network, which moves money seamlessly at the speed of light.

The Lightning Network

Money at the Speed of Light

The Lightning Network *is* Bitcoin. It offers a fast, frictionless payment method for its users, similar to credit cards. With the Lightning Network, you can send Bitcoin instantly and nearly for free—if not free, then for fractions of a penny—anywhere in the world. Bitcoin is an open, secure, permissionless system. This means anyone can create or download a bitcoin wallet to send or receive bitcoin. Anyone can use Bitcoin and the Lightning Network without permission regardless of where they live or their economic situation.

Money around the world currently operates in closed systems. Consider Venmo, PayPal, Zelle, and Revolut. All of these companies and systems can only send money within their own network. You can't send money from Venmo to Zelle or from Zelle to PayPal; transactions must occur within the same system. If someone in the U.S. wants to send dollars or any other paper currency to someone in Zimbabwe, it would be nearly impossible short of physically transporting the money to them and somehow making it through customs unscathed.

Sending money internationally is nearly impossible without using a third party, which adds additional costs and requires long processing times. For example, using a service like Western Union to send money from the U.S. to Mexico can cost up to $45 in transfer fees, *plus* any exchange or bank fees, and the settlement can still take up to five days.[1] Fees can be much higher for other currencies. The bank fee alone is over 10% when sending money to Afghanistan. By the time you factor in transfer and exchange fees, the end recipient receives only a fraction of what was sent.[2] Even bank-to-bank transfers within the U.S. can take up to five business days to settle or may not be interconnected at all. As a business owner, I've constantly struggled to send money bank to bank in the U.S.

Today, there are companies utilizing the Lightning Network as the payment infrastructure to instantly bridge between currencies.[3] Someone in the U.S. could send $100 over the Lightning Network using the app *Strike*, and a second later, someone in Mexico could receive the equivalent amount in pesos. The final settlement occurs in just a second, and the fees might equate to less than a penny. Bitcoin and the Lightning Network is the highly liquid, open network in between that allows this to happen.

Western Union, one of the largest international money transmitters that exist today, generated $4.35 billion in 2023 in revenue from fees and over $5 billion in 2021.[4] Anyone sending money home to their family is losing a significant chunk of their earnings by using such predatory services.

I believe Bitcoin and the Lightning Network is the open system we need to fix this. Imagine if value could be transferred instantly and seamlessly all over the world. We live in a global society, and we need a form of money that matches our needs.

If a business owner accepts credit cards as payment, the credit card companies charge 3% or more for each transaction. However, if a business were to accept bitcoin using the Lightning Network, this fee could be reduced to almost nothing. They could even offer a 2% discount to customers for using the Lightning Network and still save money. Additionally, while credit card payments can take 2-5 business days to settle, the Lightning Network settles instantly.

The Lightning Network

FEATURES	LIGHTNING NETWORK	CREDIT CARDS	BANKS	PAPER CURRENCY $
Settlement Time	INSTANT	2-5 BUSINESS DAYS	2-5 BUSINESS DAYS	INSTANT
Transaction Fee	NEAR 0%	3%	$15-50 (wire transfer)	$0
Chargebacks	0%	.6%	1% (bounced checks)	0%
System	OPEN	CLOSED	CLOSED	EITHER OPEN OR CLOSED (location dependent)
Global Access	YES	NO	NO	NO
Digitally Native	YES	YES	IN BETWEEN ANALOG AND DIGITAL	NO

Figure 1.1

With the Lightning Network, you can instantly buy a coffee using bitcoin with nearly zero fees. Before Lightning was implemented, spending bitcoin took an average of 10 minutes and the fees were higher for small payments. All transactions took place on the main chain, which is optimized for security, not for fast payments. Lightning introduced a second layer to be built on top of this secure model, optimizing for instant payments while still using the underlying asset—bitcoin. The internet is constructed in a similar fashion, having a secure first layer (TCP/IP) on which everything else is built—such as websites.

Some other cool ways people are using Lightning is by "streaming sats." Let's back up. What is a "sat?" One bitcoin can be divided into 100 million pieces called satoshis, also known as "sats." On the Lightning Network, sats can be divided even further into 1,000 units called millisats. At the time of writing this, 1 cent is equivalent to 15 sats or 15,000 millisats [5]

When the price of bitcoin reaches $1 million per coin, **1 sat** will equal **1 cent**.

Micropayments

Companies such as Fountain Podcasts utilize the Lightning Network to offer a platform where creators can upload their podcasts. Users are able to "stream sats" as payment for listening, and have the option to choose the number of sats they wish to stream—for instance, they can decide to stream 5 sats for every minute of listening. This way, listeners can send their favorite creators a few pennies' worth of sats in appreciation of their content. Additionally, listeners have the opportunity to earn sats by opting in to advertisements.

How many times have you encountered a paywall? You try to read an article or watch a video, only to find yourself forced into subscribing for a month or a year, undergoing a lengthy and expensive sign-up process, just to read one article —all while being bombarded with advertisements. Streaming sats can fix this. What if these paywalls said, "For every 1 minute you spend reading this article or watching this video, you must stream 10 sats." Wouldn't you be more inclined to read the article or watch a video for less than a penny? You could integrate a Lightning wallet into your web browser and set it up as your streaming wallet. By funding this wallet with $5 worth of sats, you could access content for weeks. Through these micropayments, authors get paid, and more people are encouraged to read, watch, listen, or share their work, and it can be an alternative to advertising revenue.

Micropayments can also revolutionize social media. Did someone post something that you love? Tip them a sat. Open sourced social media protocols like Nostr have already integrated this feature. Watched an incredible YouTube video? Tip them 100 sats.

Lightning has fixed not only local payments for goods and services but also global and digital payments over the internet. It puts the power back in the hands of the user without having to go through costly intermediaries. Lightning offers an updated, faster, and cheaper system for a global economy. In a world where messages and information travel the globe in seconds, Lightning ensures our money moves as quickly as our words.

Chapter 2

Bitcoin Mining and Energy

FUD #2:
Bitcoin uses too much energy/using energy is bad.

What if I told you Bitcoin could bring about cheap, abundant, renewable power for the planet? That sounds pretty good, right? Bear with me as I give a very brief background on mining without getting too deep in the technical weeds.

Bitcoin miners, also known as Application-Specific Integrated Circuits (ASICs), are just computers designed for a single purpose. They secure the Bitcoin network by applying their computing power to guessing random, very large numbers, a process known as hashing. If a computer guesses, or "hashes," the correct number, they get paid in bitcoin. By hashing that number correctly, they find the next block in the chain which rewards them with a block subsidy and the fees from transactions included in that block. Although their activity involves "guessing" numbers, their approach to finding the correct number is systematic.

The miner then transmits the new block to the network. The network consists of hundreds of thousands of users worldwide running Bitcoin nodes—computers running the Bitcoin software known as Bitcoin Core. The block transmitted by the miner is then verified by the Bitcoin nodes

Bitcoin Mining and Energy

to ensure it meets the required criteria and that all transactions included in the block are valid.

Bitcoin is an open network, meaning anyone can run a node on their computer or plug in an ASIC to mine Bitcoin. Miners are usually part of mining pools that combine their hash power to receive smaller payouts more frequently, similar to pooling together on a lottery ticket. When the pool successfully mines a block, the reward is divided among the pool members according to the amount of hash power each contributed. This allows individual miners to receive more predictable and frequent payouts compared to mining alone.

Satoshi Nakamoto, Bitcoin's anonymous creator, referred to the blockchain as a "timechain." Every 10 minutes on average, another block is found and timestamped and added to the timeline. The blockchain contains a record of every Bitcoin block mined since inception, with each block containing all the transactions for that moment in time.

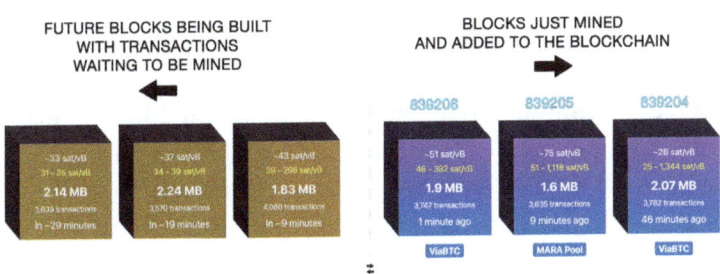

Figure 2.1 Source: mempool.space

You can look back through time and see for yourself at timechaincalendar.com or view live blocks being mined at mempool.space.

Millions of miners across the globe are hashing an extraordinarily high number of guesses every second. This hashing is Bitcoin's security system and requires an enormous amount of power. No one can break the rules of Bitcoin because of this security system. The security of Bitcoin increases with the hashrate and the global distribution of this hashrate—the more people guessing these very large, random numbers worldwide, the more secure the blockchain becomes. This is because altering any information on the blockchain would require an attacker to redo the work of mining, not just the latest block, but all subsequent blocks at a pace faster than the rest of the network. This would require an immense amount of computational power, exceeding 50% of the current global hashrate, also known as a "51% attack." A high hashrate makes this kind of attack impractically expensive and nearly impossible. We'll get into the 51% attack later in this chapter.

The global hash distribution enables resistance against state or geopolitical attacks. Should a country attempt to ban or suppress regional Bitcoin miners, these individuals are likely to relocate to more favorable jurisdictions, as was observed during the brief China mining ban in 2021.[6] A lot of the hashrate migrated to Texas and Kazakhstan during this short period, known by some as "The Great Hash Migration,"[7]

This is Bitcoin's hashrate over time:

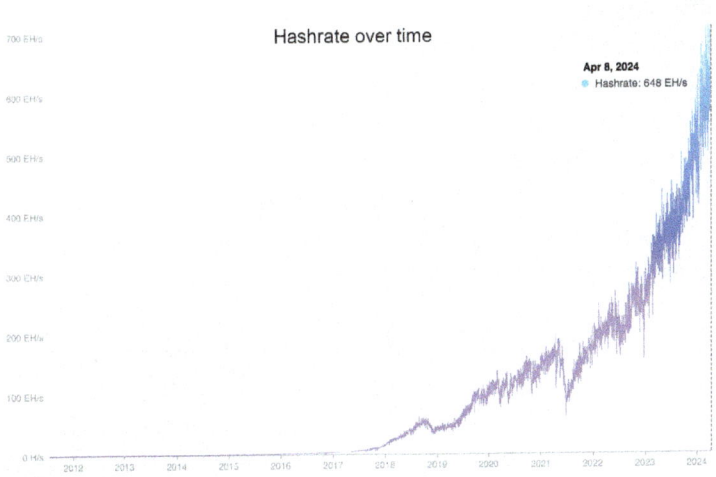

Figure 2.2 Source: mempool.space[8]

Bitcoin's global hashrate is right around 600 exahashes per second, or 600 quintillion guesses per second around the writing of this book. All of these hashes require an expenditure of energy and incur real-world costs. Miners must purchase ASICs and pay for their power consumption. This expenditure of effort to find the correct number and achieve consensus within the network is known as proof of work.

Let's explore how Bitcoin can help create affordable energy and reduce greenhouse gas emissions by capturing methane that would otherwise escape into the atmosphere.

Stranded Energy

Bitcoin mining is a highly competitive industry, and miners must seek the lowest-cost electricity to be profitable. The lowest-cost electricity tends to be from renewable and/or stranded energy sources. This energy is often cheap, free, or in some cases, miners might even get paid to use the energy.

Stranded energy refers to energy that is produced but cannot be consumed because it is generated in remote areas away from electrical grids and human populations. Many renewable energy sources, such as wind, hydropower, geothermal, and solar, are sometimes considered stranded energy. This energy is "stranded" because transmitting that energy is not cost-effective or is technically challenging. Stranded energy can also refer to untapped energy resources. For example, hydropower from a waterfall deep in the jungle, geothermal energy from a geyser in a secluded mountain area, or natural gas from an offshore oil well, all go untapped without the necessary infrastructure to capture, transport, and utilize this energy.

Oil Wells

Methane accounts for roughly 25% of the warming effect of greenhouse gases on our planet.[9] Methane is a powerful greenhouse gas that traps heat at a rate 84 times greater than CO_2 over the first 20 years, and 28 times greater than CO_2 over the following 100 years as it breaks down.

Oil wells emit methane as a byproduct of their operations. In the U.S. alone, there are approximately 1 million active oil wells and an additional 2-3 million abandoned oil wells emitting methane.[10]

If an oil well is near a populated area, oil producers have the capability to sell the methane produced back to the power grid in the form of electricity. Unfortunately, this practice is not common. Many of these active and abandoned wells are leaking methane at an alarming rate. The U.S. Environmental Protection Agency (EPA) estimates among the 2-3 million abandoned sites, 280,000 metric tons of methane are released each year, equivalent to the greenhouse gas emissions of 1.7 million cars. At many operational oil well sites, methane is flared, meaning it is burned off and released as CO_2, a less potent greenhouse gas. The average CO_2 conversion efficiency rate of flaring is 91%, meaning the other 9% of methane still escapes into the atmosphere.[11]

A study published in the journal *Science* found poor flaring performance in oil and gas production is responsible for generating excess methane pollution every year, equivalent to the climate impact of approximately 8.8 million cars.[12] Los Angeles is home to 7.5 million cars—the city with the highest number of cars in the U.S.[13] Overall, the EPA estimates that about 6.5 million metric tons of methane leak from the oil and gas supply chains in the U.S. each year, equivalent to the emissions from over 136 million cars, or half of all the cars in the U.S. today.[14,15]

Landfills

While oil wells account for 32% of all methane emissions in the U.S., landfills account for more than 14%.[16] A recent aerial survey showed over half of all landfills in the U.S. were leaking methane.[17] The U.S. has 3,000 active landfills and 10,000 closed landfills, all contributing to methane emissions, with the closed sites potentially emitting methane for 30+ years.[18]

Landfills have the same potential as oil wells to convert methane into electricity and connect it to the power grid that feeds into people's homes, or burn it off by flaring. Data is lacking for what percentage of landfills actually do this, but given over half are leaking methane, I would guess the methane mitigation is far from optimal.

Oil wells and landfills are *supposed* to flare methane. This doesn't always happen. Even when flaring is implemented, the setup costs can reach millions of dollars. The EPA has a difficult time enforcing regulations for methane mitigation and many landfill and oil companies would rather pay fines than invest millions in flaring infrastructure.

Enter Bitcoin miners. Bitcoin miners have a unique ability to be mobile power consumers, actively chasing the cheapest power. They can set up shop at remote oil wells or landfills, converting otherwise wasted methane into electricity to power their mining operations. Most importantly, the miners use electric generators to convert methane into CO_2 at a 99.89% efficiency rate compared to the 91% rate of traditional flaring methods.[19]

Oil and landfill companies are incentivized to partner with Bitcoin miners as a cost-effective, if not profitable, solution to their methane emissions problem. For the first time in history, it's possible to monetize the removal of methane from abandoned and stranded sources, all thanks to Bitcoin.

Bitcoin Mining and Energy

This chart illustrates how, rather than flaring methane from an oil well, you can channel it into a generator to create electricity that fuels the Bitcoin mining process:

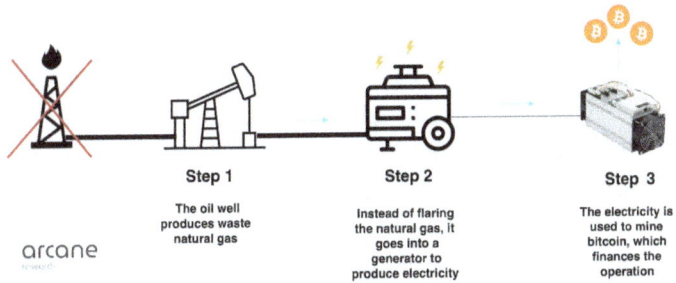

Figure 2.3 Source: Arcane Research "How Bitcoin Mining Can Transform the Energy Industry"[20]

Or, channel that electricity into the grid if you're not in a remote location.

Landfill waste → Methane extraction → Gas engine & electric generator → Grid → Homes and businesses use the electricity

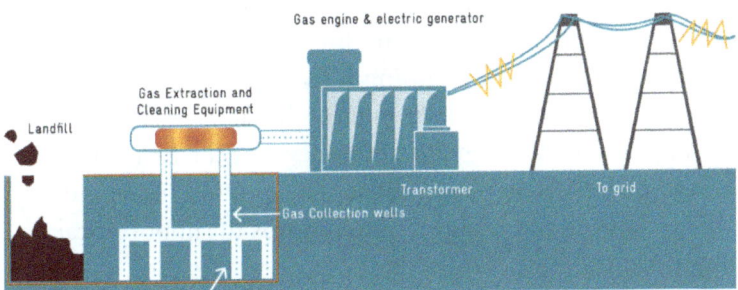

Figure 2.4 Source: Research Gate "Components of landfill gas system with energy production"[21]

A 2022 White House report on mining and climate states, "Mining operations that capture vented methane to produce electricity can yield positive results for the climate, by converting the potent methane to $CO2$ during combustion."[22]

Energy Infrastructure

In 2021, 43% of Africans (around 600 million people) did not have access to electricity. The lack of infrastructure to remote villages, inadequate funds, and ongoing corruption are responsible for this staggering number. Bitcoin mining can fix this.

Enter Gridless, a company tapping into remote hydro, geothermal, and biomass sources in Africa. They are able to channel this renewable energy into micro-grids, creating small-scale power networks that operate independently from the main grid to distribute electricity to localized areas. These projects are funded through Bitcoin mining, utilizing the surplus energy and creating consistent demand—often referred to as a buyer of last resort. The mined Bitcoin contributes to financing the construction and upkeep of these micro-grids.

Micro-grids provide affordable electricity, jobs, and often infrastructure such as roads and internet connectivity to these remote populations. By mining Bitcoin, Gridless is able to monetize building out these micro-grids all over Africa, turning stranded energy into currency. For the first time, energy companies are incentivized to tap into these remote energy sources and build out micro-grids to support local populations.

From Gridless:

Bitcoin Mining and Energy

> There is immense demand for reliable, clean, and affordable energy across Africa, yet mini-grid energy generators struggle for sustainability. Gridless works with renewable, rural, mini-grid energy generators to monetize the full capacity of their output as a buyer of last resort, as well as serving as an anchor tenant for new energy generation creation.[23]

Virunga National Park, the oldest National Park in Africa, is using Bitcoin miners to help fund operations at a chocolate factory. The World Economic Forum reports, "The mine is powered by clean energy from Virunga's 3 hydroelectric power plants. Its excess electricity is used by the factory to process cocoa beans…while the bitcoins it mines pay for salaries and infrastructure. The chocolate factory trains and employs local workers."[24]

Before Bitcoin mining, there wasn't enough electricity demand from these locations to justify the cost of building micro-grids. As a mobile buyer of last resort, Bitcoin miners can now consume all the unused energy. This breakthrough not only makes the construction of micro-grids both cost-effective and profitable, but also expands the reach of affordable electricity to more regions, providing vital economic opportunities for the community.

There's a direct correlation between per capita energy consumption and improvements in human well-being, as evidenced by longer life spans and increased gross domestic product (GDP).[25,26] The secondary benefits of solving electricity access include: improving infrastructure such as roads and internet access, and providing jobs to local populations.

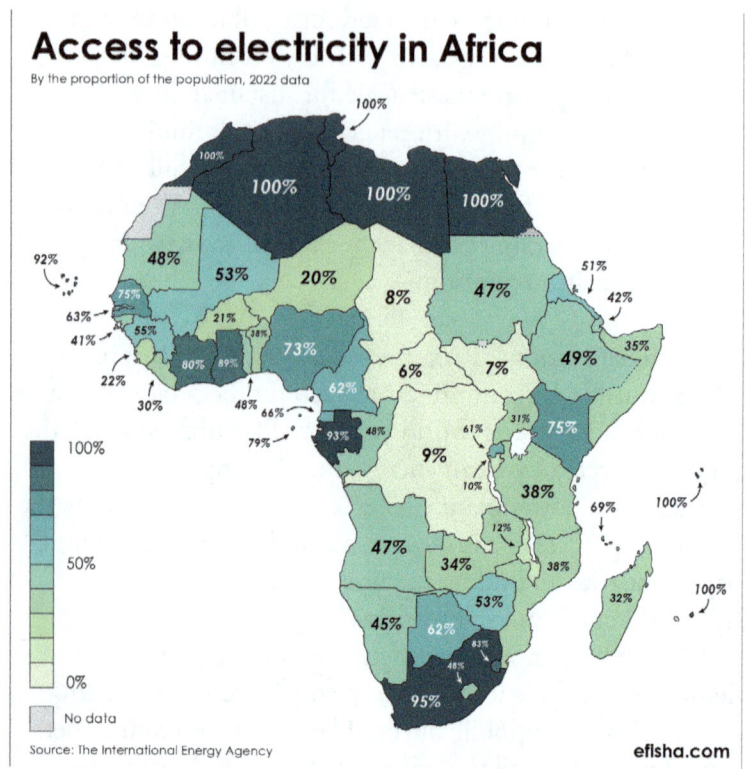

Figure 2.5 Source: The International Energy Agency. Illustrated by efisha.com.[27]

Grids
The Great Texas Freeze

In February 2021, Texas faced three major winter storms that triggered the largest failure of the state's energy infrastructure in its history. This crisis left 4.5 million homes and businesses without power, leading to shortages of food, water, and heat. At least 246 people died.

The main reasons for this failure were the lack of proper power plant winterization and the grid's inability to handle the excess demand for power necessary to heat homes in freezing temperatures. Contrary to initial reports, renewable energy sources were not the cause of the crisis; renewables remained operational throughout the storms.[28]

Rolling blackouts occur daily around the world due to poor grid infrastructure that cannot generate enough energy or adapt to fluctuating demand levels. These challenges are further exacerbated by extreme weather conditions, such as intense heat or extreme cold, often resulting in deaths.

Since those February storms in 2021, Texas has experienced a significant influx of Bitcoin miners from around the world, attracted by the cheap wind and solar energy opportunities in East Texas. This migration has led to an overbuilding of power generation beyond typical demand needs, enabling greater flexibility in usage, especially during storms. In response to periods of high energy demand, miners have the capability to instantly power down their ASICs, rerouting electricity back to the grid in real time. Texas power companies are incentivized to produce more power as there is now a buyer of last resort— the Bitcoin miners.

This dynamic enables increased energy generation and the expansion of grid infrastructure to reliably meet power requirements, regardless of demand fluctuations. No more rolling blackouts, no more power insecurity, no more unnecessary deaths.

> "Bitcoin miners can use excess power overnight and on days where demand is normal, and they can turn off on very hot or very cold days when power is scarce and electricity prices are high."
>
> -Lee Bratcher, President of the Texas Blockchain Council[29]

Intro to Bitcoin

In August 2023, Bitcoin mining company Riot Platforms reported they had turned off 95% of their miners during the summer's harshest heatwaves.[30] This action helps prevent rolling blackouts or scheduled brownouts, which might occur when consumption exceeds generation capacity.

Companies like Riot have even negotiated for demand response credits as part of their power agreements. This is because they're getting paid by the power companies for not using electricity. If miners have to shut off to curtail power needs for the grid, they can remain profitable even without mining Bitcoin. These types of demand response agreements allow not only miners, but utility companies to more effectively plan and manage their operations.

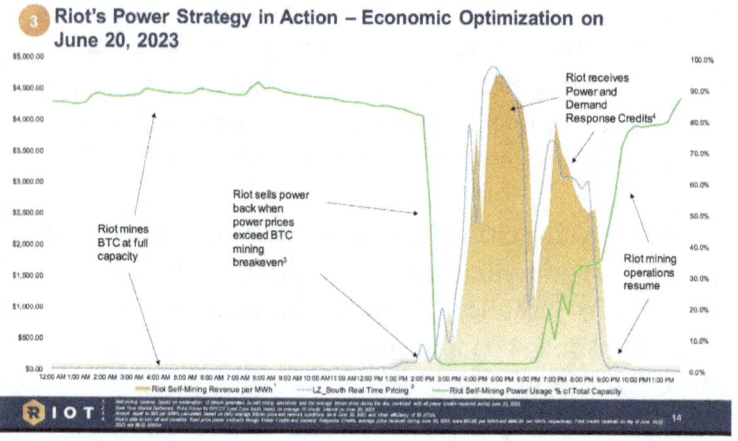

Figure 2.6 Source: Riot[31]

Intermittent energy sources, such as solar and wind, have traditionally been troublesome for grids because they only generate power when the sun shines or wind blows. What happens when this power is generated during periods of low demand? Traditionally, it would go to waste. Now, with

Bitcoin mining acting as a buyer of last resort, there is a flexible demand for this power. This dynamic enables the expansion of renewable energy sources, making them more viable and profitable by ensuring there's always a market for the electricity they generate.

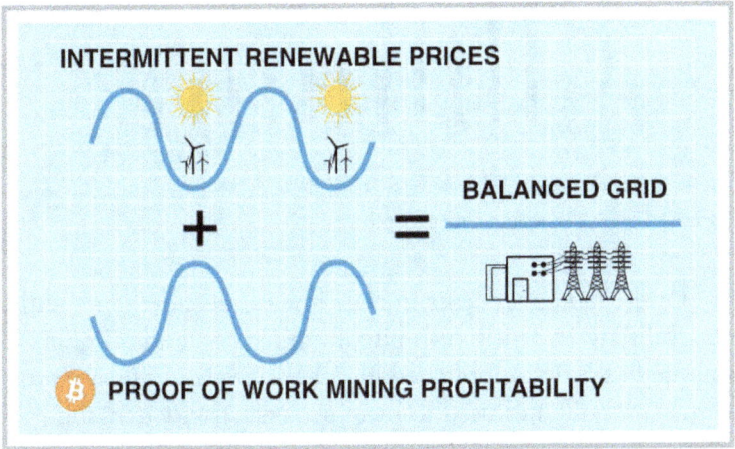

Figure 2.7 Source: @level39[32]

The Bitcoin mining council (BMC) reported 59.9% of global Bitcoin miners are using a sustainable power mix.[33] Due to their adaptability, Bitcoin miners chase the cheapest forms of energy, which tend to be renewable sources. As a result, miners use a higher percentage of renewable energy compared to other industries or countries.

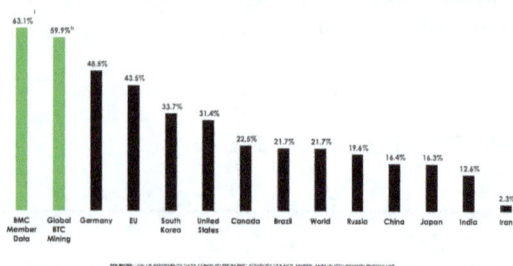

Figure 2.8 Source: Bitcoin Mining Council[34]

Grid balancing occurs in real-time to meet demand, and the ability to instantly turn bitcoin miners on and off offers unique flexibility unmatched by other systems. Peaker plants, which are built and used to meet peak electricity demand, primarily utilize expensive natural gas, sit idle most of the time and are only activated during periods of high demand. A 2020 report revealed that over the previous ten years, New Yorkers had paid over $4.5 billion to maintain the city's peaker plants, despite their limited operation of just 90 to 500 hours annually—less than three weeks at most. Consequently, the cost for peak electricity in New York City was a staggering 1,300 percent higher than the state's average electricity cost.[35] These plants also release dangerous pollutants such as sulfur dioxide, nitrogen oxides, and fine particulate matter into nearby communities, which are often low-income neighborhoods of color. Overbuilding the grid with renewables and other resources to exceed demand means there is no need to construct these costly peaker plants. Additionally, as battery technology advances, batteries offer not only a cost advantage but also much faster response times; they can ramp up and down instantly in response to signals from the grid operator, a flexibility and responsiveness similar to Bitcoin miners that gas peakers cannot match.

The traditional gas peaker plants are designed to supplement underbuilt grid capacity and activate only when there's a spike in electricity demand, for instance, when A/C usage increases on a hot day. Due to fluctuating energy use and generation, renewables paired with batteries necessitate an overbuilding of generation capacity to ensure sufficient energy storage for later use. However, this often leads to production exceeding what battery storage can handle, making Bitcoin miners the perfect candidate to absorb the excess energy that would otherwise be wasted.

Low-Grade Heat

Computers produce heat as a waste product. Your laptop produces heat. Servers in data centers produce heat. 100% of the electricity consumed by a computer ends up as excess heat. ASICs are no exception. There are millions of ASICs all over the world producing mass amounts of heat that is not being utilized. What if you could repurpose that wasted heat? What if there was a monetary incentive to harness that heat and put it to use?

Right now, my apartment and my hot tub are currently heated with ASICs. I call my hot tub the "Hot Tub Mine Machine." The bitcoin I receive from mining helps offset my electricity bill. My bill is around the same price as it was using traditional electric heating, except now, I'm earning bitcoin. If you are currently heating with electricity anyway, why not get paid to do so?

> "The heat from your computer is not wasted if you need to heat your home."
>
> - Satoshi Nakamoto

ASICs are currently being used to heat homes, buildings, pools and bathhouses. People have also gotten creative with how to use this excess heat for food dehydration, including drying fruits and chocolates. For instance, the same Virunga National Park that uses excess energy from hydroelectric power plants to fund their chocolate factory operations with Bitcoin miners, is now preparing to use the surplus heat generated by their miners for drying chocolate. This approach effectively takes waste and turns it into a profit.

Alex Gladstein, Director of the Human Rights Foundation, posted:

> Currently the cocoa is sun-dried, taking 3 weeks. Instead of buying an industrial dryer for $200k, the park bought ASICs which will reduce the time to 1 week. Soon they'll dry the cocoa with hydro-powered BTC mining.[36]

There have also been reports of using excess ASIC heat to dry clothes and wood, as well as using that heat in maple syrup and whisky distillation.[37,38, 39,40] This wasted heat presents an additional revenue stream. Every home, office, commercial or industrial building, food drying or electric powered laundry facility could be a beneficiary of this wasted heat. Today, you can replace the electric space heater in your home with an ASIC for $200.

It's this sort of outside-the-box thinking that has brought about some of the greatest breakthroughs in technology across industries. The concept of using waste heat has potential applications beyond Bitcoin mining. While data centers traditionally haven't utilized their waste heat, they could adopt and profit from this practice. It often takes those operating on the margins, like Bitcoin miners, who are driven to maximize every resource, to lead the way in discovering crafty repurposing solutions such as this.

> "Bitcoin generation should end up where it's cheapest. Maybe that will be in cold climates where there's electric heat, where it would be essentially free."
>
> -Satoshi Nakamoto, 2010

Bitcoin mining may be the answer to securing a more abundant, reliable, and environmentally sustainable energy future for our planet. Increased energy production and enhanced grid infrastructure contribute to human flourishing by lifting people out of poverty. The ability of miners to instantly turn on and off helps balance the grid, preventing blackouts and reducing reliance on expensive, environmentally damaging gas peaker plants. Access to power not only boosts productivity but also supports the development of critical infrastructure, such as internet connectivity and transportation networks. Furthermore, mining helps to subsidize energy costs, enabling more people to access and afford essential energy resources. The presence of miners as a guaranteed buyer of last resort encourages the development of renewable energy sources, funding the necessary infrastructure. Bitcoin mining also monetizes capturing stranded energy sources such as leaking methane from oil wells and landfills, lowering their overall carbon footprint. Additionally, the low-grade heat produced by miners can be harnessed and utilized anywhere electric heat is needed.

Essentially, **NOT** mining Bitcoin wastes energy.

Energy Use
Now, let's address the "using energy is bad" FUD.

We know Bitcoin uses a lot of energy. But is using energy inherently bad? Can you impose moral standards on energy consumption? "I think reality TV is worthless, and you should not be allowed to waste electricity watching it." "You're using too many Christmas lights and wasting energy." "Running a washing machine is wasteful because it consumes too much energy; so you should wash your clothes by hand instead." "Storing data on the cloud is wasteful because it requires too much electricity to run the servers." "Flying, driving, or traveling at all is a waste of energy, so everyone should just stay home…forever."

Calling energy consumption wasteful is a slippery slope backwards in time. What one individual defines as wasteful or bad may vary from person to person. Human progress requires energy. An increase in energy consumption per capita has been linked to improvements in human well-being and life expectancy.[41] We also explored how Bitcoin mining can help monetize energy abundance, the development of renewables, and infrastructure to lift people out of poverty.

Not only does Bitcoin provide an open, permissionless, superior monetary network to the world, but it also positively impacts humans and our planet through these energy ripple effects.

Furthermore, advancements in chip technology are enhancing the efficiency of Bitcoin miners each year, reducing the energy required to secure a higher hashrate. Simply put, securing the same amount of hashrate now requires fewer ASICs and less power.

This chart shows the global energy consumption of our current banking system, gold mining, and Bitcoin mining as of May 2021:

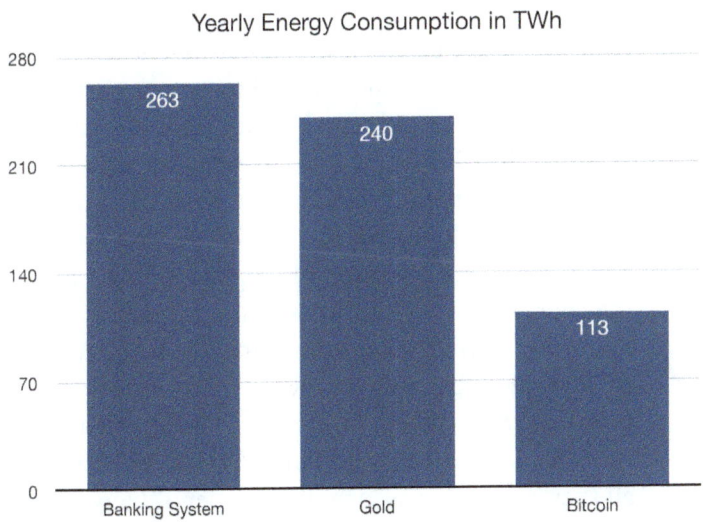

Figure 2.9 Source: Galaxy Digital May 2021 Report[42]

FUD #3:
The 51% Attack

A theoretical 51% attack could happen if one bad actor controlled 51% or more of the Bitcoin hashrate.

Intro to Bitcoin

I'm going to let the great Andreas Antonopoulos, an early Bitcoin educator, take this one. During a talk in 2015, when the Bitcoin network's hashrate was just .05% of what it is today in 2024, Andreas took a question about a 51% attack:

> **Question**: Do you have any concerns about a large nation state that has interest in just actively destroying Bitcoin to make their own super rigs and design chips and just throw hundreds of millions or billions of dollars to intentionally disrupt the blockchain?
>
> **Andreas**: Yeah, I don't worry about that at all. This cannot be done with Bitcoin anymore. This is something that can only be done with nascent altcoins. Bitcoin has achieved a level of computing that no single nation state can overthrow it through computation alone. The effort to do so would require a massive covert operation of chip fabrication then the coordinated assault that would give them dominance over the next block for 10 minutes, until we kick those bastards off the network, rework the protocol around them. They would be revealed, they would have lost a billion dollars doing this and all they got to do was one double spend. Now here's the thing, long before we get to that point, they figure out that if they just let this stuff run, they can actually get some bitcoin as a reward, because the incentive structure actually works and so I'm not worried about that.[43]

Again, this took place when the hashrate of the network was .05% of what it is today. The amount of energy resources one would need to secure to expend enough energy to attack the network, the amount of chip fabrication, and the incredible amount of secrecy to pull this off is likely impossible, and only gets more impossible as the Bitcoin network grows. The market for Bitcoin ASICs in 2022 alone was nearly $9 billion.[44] The entire Bitcoin network uses around 20 gigawatts of energy today. In 2023, Michael Saylor, the founder of MicroStrategy, compared the Bitcoin network, then at only 10 gigawatts, to the U.S. Navy fleet:

> The United States Navy has 53 Virginia-class attack submarines that have 30 megawatts each. It has 14 Ohio-class ballistic missile submarines that have about 45 megawatts of power each. It has 11 nuclear powered aircraft carriers with about 195 megawatts of power each from their nuclear reactors. It's got 17 cruisers that run about 60 megawatts each, and 62 destroyers that have something like 30 megawatts each. When you add it all up, the entire Navy, the nuclear Navy is running like 4.3 gigawatts of power…you know we used to say that the U.S. dollar is backed by the strength of the U.S. Navy, by the power of the Navy. Well, it is; and now you know what the Navy is. The Navy isn't 10 gigawatts. Bitcoin is 10.6 gigawatts; it's like double the energy that powers the entire U.S. Navy. Another way to think of it: as a full on nuclear power plant might generate a gigawatt, a massive one. It's like 10.5 full on nuclear power plants running all out, but it's better because it's distributed everywhere in the grid and you can't identify where that energy (comes from). It's more distributed than the Navy, it's more distributed than a nuclear power plant. You can't stop it.[45]

The Bitcoin network could now have the energy of 5 U.S. Navy fleets. The amount of energy alone required to pull this off makes a 51% attack purely theoretical. However, securing and controlling the supply of ASICs is by far the most prohibitive aspect of this theoretical attack.

To clarify Andreas's point that "all they got to do was one double spend:" a double spend means managing to use the same coins for two separate transactions. Let's say the attacker had 1,000 bitcoin. If they were able to muster up enough hashrate to dominate the network, which realistically requires controlling well over 51% of it, they could spend their bitcoin twice. However, the cost of such an attack would be an order of magnitude higher than the potential profit. Bitcoin's incentive system is designed to deter attacks, making it more profitable for someone to join the network as a good actor and receive bitcoin as reward for their contributed hashrate.

Chapter 3

Financial Independence and Human Rights

This chapter gives a quick look at how Bitcoin can support human rights and foster financial independence. We'll explore some of these topics in greater detail throughout the book.

Many people in Western countries overlook the advantages that come with being born into a liberal democracy. These benefits include property rights, freedom of speech, access to a stable reserve currency like the dollar or pound, and the presence of a functioning legal system.

Around 54% of the world's population, over 4 billion people, live under authoritarian regimes today, and 1.6 billion people live under double or triple digit inflation.[46,47]

Banking the Unbanked

The World Bank estimates 1.4 billion people around the world are unbanked today, meaning they lack access to fundamental financial tools and resources such as savings accounts, loans, and insurance. The absence of these services not only hinders personal financial growth and stability but also obstructs economic development in underprivileged regions.[48]

Even in the United States, The Federal Reserve's 2019 data indicates about 22% of American adults, or 63 million people, were classified as either unbanked or underbanked. Of this group, 6% of Americans had no bank account at all, relying instead on alternative financial options such as payday loans, check-cashing services, money orders, and loans from pawn shops for managing their finances. The remaining 16% were underbanked, meaning they had a bank account but still utilized these alternative services to meet their financial needs.

Bitcoin may provide opportunities and financial security to some of the most vulnerable people in society. Here are a few examples:

Women's Rights

Imagine a woman living in the Republic of Congo. She cannot get a bank account without her husband's permission. She cannot enter into any legally binding contract such as owning property or starting a business without permission from her husband. Her husband has full control over her assets. If she wanted to leave, what options would she have?

Roya Mahboob, recognized as the first female tech CEO from Afghanistan and listed among TIME's most influential people, was one of the first entrepreneurs to introduce Bitcoin to Afghanistan. She was only seven years old when the Taliban first invaded her hometown in 1996. In 2013, she began paying employees and contractors in bitcoin, and "the girls were happy to finally have a money that the men in their lives could not take from them," she said. "It gave them security, privacy and peace of mind."[49]

Education and access to Bitcoin could mean the difference between being stuck in an abusive relationship to having the financial independence and privacy to leave.

Individuals can carry their bitcoin with them through private keys stored on a drive or by memorizing 12 words in their head. This method of control is crucial for many abuse victims who are often unable to escape their situations due to their captors controlling their finances.

By memorizing the 12 or 24 seed words associated with their bitcoin private key, individuals can access their bitcoin on any bitcoin wallet. Wherever internet access is available, they can recover their bitcoin, whether by using a secure hardware device—a cold wallet (offline), or a hot wallet (online) that connects directly to the internet, such as through a smartphone.

Refugees

For refugees, the ability to store Bitcoin in their memory represents a crucial lifeline in an otherwise turbulent journey. Fleeing from conflict, persecution, or economic instability in their home countries, traditional ways of protecting wealth often become impractical or risky. Carrying physical currency can make them vulnerable to theft or confiscation by authorities or criminals along the way. Additionally, they may fear their home currency will inflate or become non-exchangeable upon reaching their destination. By memorizing their private keys or their 12 or 24 words associated with it, refugees can securely transport their wealth across borders. These words can also be discreetly written down on a small piece of paper or saved on a thumb drive. For many refugees who have lost everything in their search for safety and freedom, Bitcoin represents more than just a digital currency—it's a means of preserving their financial stability, independence, and hope for a better future. It empowers them to rebuild their lives and support themselves and their families in the face of adversity. Bitcoin offers financial stability amid the chaos of displacement.

Activism

Another situation where freedom money proves invaluable is for activists protesting against corruption in their country, who risk having their bank accounts frozen. Given that 54% of the global population lives under authoritarian regimes, Bitcoin presents a vital alternative for these activists, allowing them to bypass conventional banking systems. There have been numerous reports of activists using Bitcoin after having their bank accounts frozen, ranging from Nigeria to Hong Kong to Belarus to Ukraine. This scenario recently unfolded in the West during the 2022 Freedom Convoy in Canada, where truckers protesting vaccine mandates saw their bank accounts suddenly frozen and turned to bitcoin donations as a lifeline.
Alex Gladstein, director of the Human Rights foundation recently stated in a *What Bitcoin Did* podcast:

> It will ultimately be impossible to keep Bitcoin out of a country. Let's say you're China or India or Russia, let's say you're the dictator of one of these countries. What do you need to survive? You need: censorship, confiscation, closed capital markets. You cannot survive without these three things. Now what is Bitcoin? Bitcoin is free speech, property rights, and open capital markets. It's fundamentally opposed to the DNA of dictatorship. Now it doesn't mean that there won't be autocrats in a Bitcoin standard, but it will be a lot harder to do so because people will have the power to push back and to be financially free and that's going to be very devastating for them.[50]

Remittance Payments

Remittance payments refer to foreign workers sending money back to individuals in their home country. These payments are a significant part of the economy in many countries, providing a crucial source of income for families, and contributing to the overall economic development. In 2023, global remittance payments were $860 billion and are projected to grow 3.1% in 2024.[51]

We already know the Bitcoin Lightning Network offers an instant, nearly free option to send value across borders without intermediaries, wait times, or predatory fees. Anyone with a smartphone with a Bitcoin or Lightning wallet can effortlessly send and receive funds globally. There are actually ways to send on SMS-only devices with an intermediary node who is connected to the internet, ensuring accessibility for those with limited internet access. As Bitcoin adoption continues to grow and more people embrace the Lightning Network, the Western Unions of the world are facing a disruption to their long-established dominance and excessive fees.

Asset Seizure

In 2012-2013, Cyprus faced an economic crisis. This was largely due to its banks' overextension of credit, particularly to Greek government bonds and local real estate sectors. The losses from Greek bond holdings contributed significantly to Cyprus's financial turmoil, leading to the downgrade of its government bond credit rating to junk. On March 25, 2013, Cyprus was offered a €10 billion bailout. However, this financial rescue came with strict conditions: Cyprus had to shut down its second-largest bank, the Cyprus Popular Bank, and seize around 48% of all accounts holding over €100,000 in both the Cyprus Popular Bank and the Bank of Cyprus, the island's largest commercial bank.[52,53]

Citizens woke up to the news in a panic upon discovering their banks were closed and ATMs were offline leaving them powerless to withdraw their money. The government had stolen their life savings. There was no recourse. Their money was just gone.

Alex Gladstein's book, *Check Your Financial Privilege*, features multiple stories of individuals around the globe turning to Bitcoin as a means to escape broken financial systems and protect their wealth from confiscation. Gladstein provides an account of such an incident in Sudan:

> On top of what was taken through traditional taxation and seigniorage, citizens had to pay a portion of their income to help the martyrs of their dictator's wars. The secret monetary police would spy on individuals, freeze bank accounts, confiscate assets, and impose made-up fees on merchants. No reasonable suspicion was required.[54]

Corrupt regimes frequently engage in asset seizures. For the 54% of people living under authoritarian regimes, Gladstein writes, "For them, Bitcoin is a protest, a lifeline, and a way out."[55]
Bitcoin is a fair monetary system based on rules. It does not cheat. It does not steal.

Escaping inflation is another way Bitcoin enables financial independence and promotes human rights. In the next chapter, we'll dive deeper into inflation and its impacts on financial freedom.

Part 2
Fiat: the Corruption Strikes Back

"You must unlearn what you have learned."

-Yoda

Bitcoin is not an intelligence test. It's an ego test. Can you unlearn what you have learned? Can you learn how our current system works and apply first principles thinking on how to make improvements? Can you adapt as new information comes to light? What is money? Who decides what money is? Why does inflation exist?

Chapter 4

Money 101

> "It is well enough that people of the nation do not understand our banking and monetary system, for if they did, I believe there would be a revolution before tomorrow morning."
>
> -Henry Ford

Fiat Currency

The word "fiat" means "by authoritative decree." Every paper currency you've ever touched has been issued by a government or central bank. Fiat currency includes dollars, pesos, euros, yen, lira, yuan, or any of the 180 government currencies that exist today. Throughout history, nearly every fiat currency has failed within 50 years. Exceptions include the U.S. dollar and the British pound. Yet, since the creation of the Federal Reserve in 1913, the dollar has lost 98% of its purchasing power, and the British pound has lost 98% of its value since 1950 alone.

When someone controls the ability to create and issue new currency, it's too easy to keep printing money. It's a temptation every government or empire has succumbed to eventually. As more currency is printed and enters the system, it makes the existing currency worth less, a.k.a. inflation. Inflation is the rise in prices and the loss of purchasing power of a currency over time. Only by having a fixed supply of money, or "hard money" that no one can manipulate, can you stop currencies from inflating. Think about it from a purchasing power point of view. How much did buying a soda cost when you were a kid? How much did your childhood home cost? What about groceries? And what do those same things cost today? Unless you're a kid today, I bet that number is multiples higher. The dollar has lost almost 98% of its purchasing power in the last 100 years.

This chart depicts the purchasing power of the U.S. dollar through 2024:

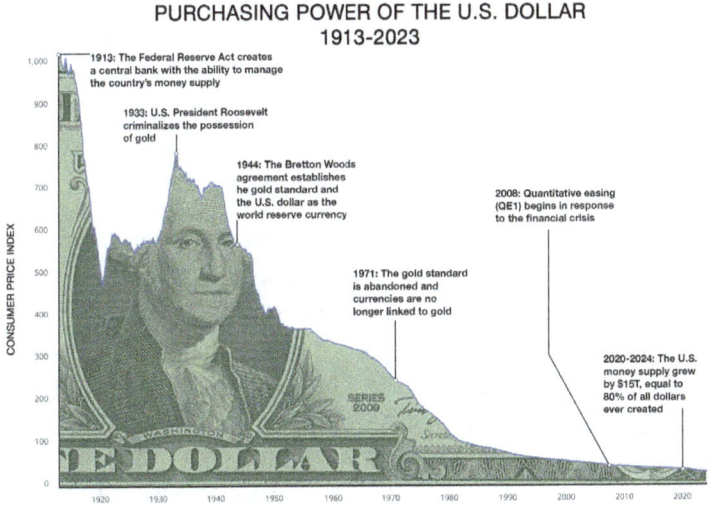

Figure 4.1 Source: Federal Bank of St. Louis[56]

This chart shows the dollars added to the system since 1960. Since 2008, around 70% of all dollars have been added to the system. Yes, 70% of all the dollars that have ever existed were created after 2008. Since 2020, around 30% of all U.S. dollars have been printed.

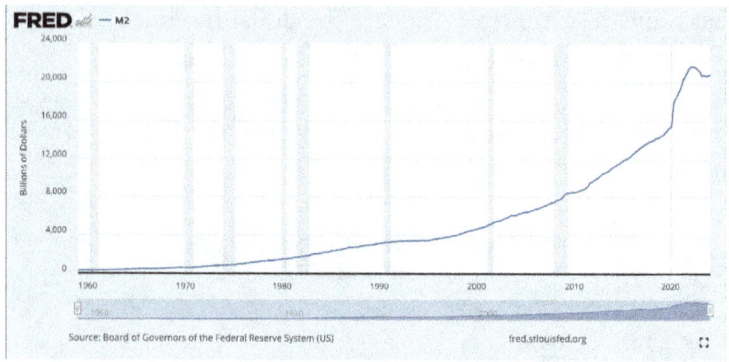

Figure 4.2 Source: Federal Bank of St. Louis[57]

This is just in the U.S. Across the world, it can be much worse. Many countries experience hyperinflation. Imagine inflation rates of 50% or more a month—how does that sound? So a house that costs you $100k today would cost $150k next month and nearly $13 million in one year. This forces people to spend their money instantly, otherwise it just melts away on a daily basis. In Argentina alone, there have been three hyperinflationary events within my lifetime.

These are the countries whose currencies have hyperinflated just in 2022-2023:

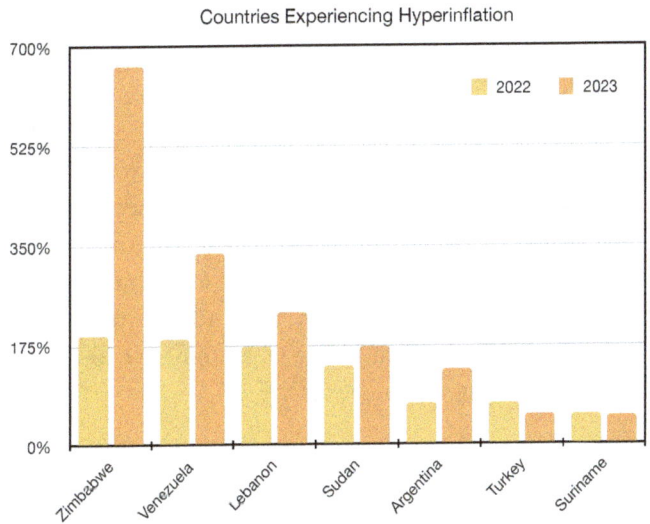

Figure 4.3 Sources: International Monetary Fund, World Bank[58,59]

Many other countries have extremely high inflation, just not at that 50% a month rate. The U.S. government measures inflation with its Consumer Price Index (CPI). Keep in mind that CPI today conveniently leaves out food, energy, and the cost of buying a home. If inflation was measured using pre-1983 housing calculations, the true inflation rate would be around 2x what is actually reported today.[60]

Life is becoming more expensive. But why? The primary driver of inflation is money printing. Governments can't spend within their means so they "print" more currency to fund their projects. Today, that printing is usually just adding more zeros on a computer screen. This process effectively steals purchasing power from citizens by flooding the system with additional units of currency. To maintain its purchasing power and avoid inflation, money must be earned through the addition of value, not simply created at will. When money is printed out of thin air rather than backed by actual work, its value depreciates over time due to increased availability and decreased scarcity. Money is supposed to be a way for humans to store the fruits of their labor today for something they need later on. Government money printing is similar to a company diluting its share value by issuing more stock, or when additional rare collectibles are produced, making the originals less valuable. The fundamental concept is the same: the more units added to a system, the less valuable each existing unit becomes.

Money is Time.

Let's say your groceries cost $100 today. If the same groceries cost $200 next year, you have to work twice as hard to buy the same items. Your wages might go up a little, but never enough to cover actual inflation. When governments add to the money supply, they're quite literally stealing time from you. Printing money doesn't add value, it steals value… it steals time.

Living in a system when the value of your work today is worth less next month, is a horrible way to live. You must have a high time preference to get through your day to day life. "I made $10 today; quick, I need to run to the store and buy bread before the price increases tomorrow." Little thought can be given to the future because it becomes impossible to preserve your wealth over time. Many people that live in high or hyperinflationary environments will have to work every day for the rest of their lives to survive. Their time is stolen from them.

Even in countries with lower rates of inflation, leaving your money in a bank means it will be worth less the following year.

Results of Inflation over Time

Inflation Rate	Years to 50% Loss in Purchasing Power
2%	36 years
4%	18 years
12%	6 years
24%	2 years

Figure 4.4

"Printing money is merely taxation in another form. Rather than robbing citizens of their money, government robs their money of its purchasing power."

- Peter Schiff

The Money Spigot

Those closest to the source of new money—the "money spigot"—invariably benefit the most from an increase in the money supply. Politicians, high net worth individuals, CEOs, Wall Street, for example, often possess assets such as real estate, stocks, and companies that appreciate in value with the printing of money. This uneven wealth distribution, known as the Cantillon Effect, enables them to weather the negative impacts of inflation. The following charts show asset prices can at least keep pace with inflation:

House prices:

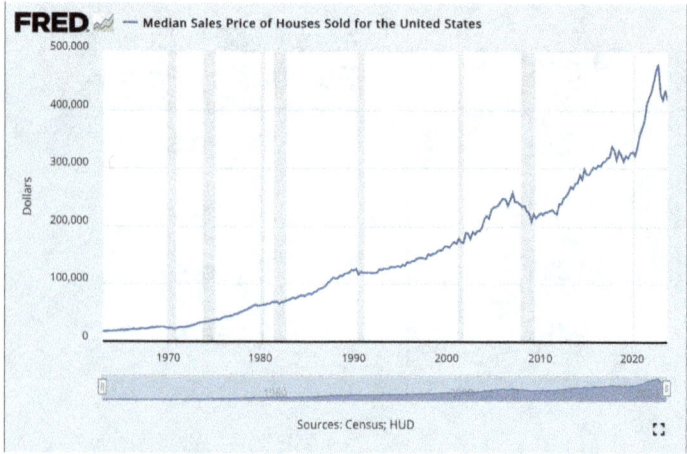

Figure 4.5 Source: Federal Bank of St. Louis[61]

Stock prices:

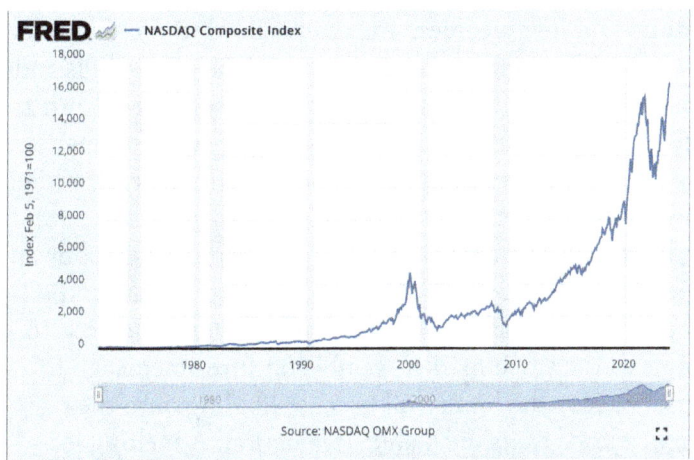

Figure 4.6 Source: Federal Bank of St. Louis[62]

Corporate Profits and the NASDAQ:

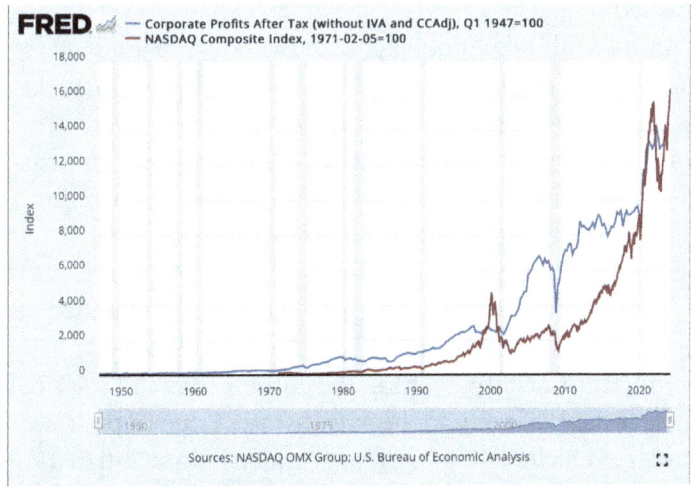

Figure 4.7 Source: Federal Bank of St. Louis[63]

Money printing disproportionately affects those with medium and low incomes. They can't afford to dump money into assets like real estate or stocks while their daily bills and living expenses keep going up in price. They're literally on a hamster wheel running faster and faster. There's nothing left over to save, they're falling more and more in debt, all while taking on second and third jobs.

Since fiat currencies do not hold their purchasing power, individuals are forced to go further and further out on the risk curve just to save for their future. They feel the need to gamble in the stock market, gamble on investments, go to a casino, or play the lottery, all because holding onto their currency leads to its inevitable devaluation. A melting ice cube, if you will. Imagine being able to store your hard work in sound money and not having to become a day trader or financial market guru just to try to beat inflation. The stress of constantly trying to retain your purchasing power can be overwhelming.

Almost half of all publicly traded U.S. companies are unprofitable. In 2018 alone, 83% of initial public stock offerings (IPOs) were filed by unprofitable companies.[64] In this fiat currency system, companies no longer need to add value to attract investment. They have become a refuge for individuals looking to preserve their wealth, since their money does not retain its purchasing power.

A great repricing would happen if the world switched to a scarce money system that could not be controlled by governments or central banks. The current prices in the stock and real estate markets are heavily distorted due to their use as savings vehicles by fiat currency holders. These inflated market valuations are not grounded in reality. Under a system where money retains its purchasing power over time, companies that do not generate real revenue would not be artificially supported by investors and would be allowed to fail.

Overall, the fair market value of many of these companies would be much lower. If a company fails to generate profits and doesn't offer a better return than simply holding onto the money, what motivation exists to invest? Investing under these circumstances would be a gamble, relying on the hope they turn things around and provide compensation for lost time.

If money actually served as a way to store time, a house would no longer be a store of value. Instead, you would buy a house just to live in, not as an investment, and its price would reflect its utility alone. The house would revert to its original purpose as a consumption item, "shelter," rather than as a store of value. The monetary premium on real estate could drop substantially as the free market repriced everything according to its utility rather than its speculative potential. Our measuring stick for what things are worth has become incredibly distorted by the money printer.

Why does money printing happen over and over again? Humans with access to the money printer can't help themselves. Let's say the U.S. wanted to go to war. How would they finance that? Let the people vote to raise taxes to fund the war? That would be wildly unpopular and would never pass. It's much easier to just print the money. That way it's slowly stealing the purchasing power away from their citizens at a rate that usually goes unnoticed. The public is paying for the war either way, printing is just a psychologically easier way to manipulate citizens and steal their time. This strategy of secretive financing through money printing has happened repeatedly throughout human history.

> "The root problem with conventional currency is all the trust that's required to make it work. The central bank must be trusted not to debase the currency, but the history of fiat currencies is full of breaches of that trust."
>
> -Satoshi

Debt

The U.S. has actually defaulted on its fiat-issued debt four times since 1862. The process of issuing debt is just another way of expanding the money supply, or "printing money," and often leads to the devaluation of the currency. With the U.S. currently over $34 trillion in debt and climbing, the interest payments on this debt alone are more than the U.S. spends on its defense budget.[65] This cycle of borrowing and printing money to finance deficits, leading to further debt, is often referred to as a "debt spiral." Think of this as using your Mastercard to pay off your Visa. Using a currency that could not be printed out of thin air might disincentivize future war. If you cannot manipulate and print more money, how would you fund war? Citizens would have to agree to spend their money, their precious stored time, to go to war.

So, the fiat currency system is broken. What is the solution?

A money that has a finite or scarce supply that no one can print more of. A money that no one can control.

Other valuable qualities of good money include verifiability, transportability, and divisibility.

One must be able to verify the money they're receiving is, in fact, legitimate—i.e., is this a counterfeit bill or is this really solid gold?

Money must be transportable so it can be delivered quickly and cheaply, i.e., can the money go from point A to point B in a reasonable amount of time without the involvement of costly intermediaries?

Money must be divisible in order to facilitate trade, i.e., can I buy a car from you today and you buy an apple from me tomorrow? For instance, if money were in the form of cows, how would we manage to make the correct change for our smaller transactions? Effective money requires units of currency that are easily divisible.

Money serves 3 functions:
Store of value
Unit of account
Medium of exchange

Gold

Gold served as the best form of money until the 20th century.
It's a durable metal that does not corrode over time, ensuring its longevity. The acquisition of gold comes at a real cost, or "work," due to the effort required to mine it from the earth. Gold's scarcity contributes to its relatively low inflation rate, meaning not a lot of gold is added to the supply each year (gold currently has a 2% supply inflation rate.) This makes gold a relatively good store of value. Chemically, gold is uniform, meaning one piece is identical to another. Gold can be divided into smaller units, such as coins or bars, enabling different size transactions to take place. Many cultures and empires valued gold throughout history, giving it an enduring medium of exchange.

Problems with Gold.

Gold cannot be transported easily. What if you want to move gold from the U.S. to Europe? You need everything from armed guards, transport trucks, and numerous forms of transportation to get there. Gold is difficult to secure. It can be confiscated or stolen from vaults and coins can be stolen from your pockets. For large quantities of gold, vaults and around the clock security details are necessary. The U.S. spends $5 million a year on Fort Knox security alone, where they "reportedly" safeguard 147.3 million troy ounces of gold.[66]

Due to these difficulties in storage and transportation, paper IOUs for gold were issued in the past, as seen in the early 20th century in the U.S.

Here is a $5 bill from 1928 that reads, "Redeemable in gold on demand at the United States Treasury, or in gold or lawful money at any federal reserve bank."

Figure 4.8 Source: Wikipedia "Series of 1928 (United States Currency)"[67]

Gold confiscation from citizens by governments has been a recurring problem throughout history. In 1933, U.S. President Franklin D. Roosevelt issued Executive Order 6102, "forbidding the hoarding of gold coin, gold bullion, and gold certificates within the continental United States." All gold held by individuals was seized at the exchange rate of

$20.67 per ounce. In 1934, the Gold Reserve Act changed the value of an ounce of gold to $35, effectively devaluing the U.S. dollar since less gold was now required to back the currency. With gold having a fixed peg to the dollar, this revision allowed for the creation of more dollars. Essentially, the U.S. government "printed" more money with a stroke of a pen, reducing its purchasing power. Sound familiar?

The Roman Empire engaged in a similar strategy of "coin clipping," or shaving bits of gold from its existing coins in order to mint new ones. This increased the supply of coins in circulation without having done the work of mining more gold. This again reduced the purchasing power of the existing coins. Prices increase as the scarcity of money decreases. Whatever form it takes throughout history, money printing inherently leads to inflation and the collapse of the currency.

The U.S. continued to print money until it became evident the dollar was not backed by the gold reserves they claimed to have. As a result, the U.S. officially abandoned the gold standard in 1971.

The dollar is now officially "backed" by nothing. It can be printed at will. No work is required to print more.

Another problem with gold is that it is difficult to verify. How do you know the bars or coins you have are solid gold? Extensive tests need to be done to verify the purity.

Figure 4.9 This image represents a "gold" bar that has a tungsten core. Because gold and tungsten have similar weights for their size, this bar looks and feels just like a solid gold bar.

Gold is not easily divisible. If all you have is one gold bar and you want to buy a loaf of bread, dividing the bar into smaller units to pay the correct amount is challenging. Additionally, attempting to divide it on the spot by shaving off a piece of the bar involves guesswork regarding the value of that shave. This is also an issue for any coined money.

Furthermore, gold mining can have devastating environmental consequences, including destruction of ecosystems, pollution, slave labor, and the displacement of communities.[68]

Properties of Bitcoin

This brings us to Bitcoin. Let's contrast Bitcoin's properties to other monetary systems.

Gold vs USD vs Bitcoin

Properties of Money	Gold	Fiat (USD)	Bitcoin
Fungibility	High	High	High
Portability	Moderate	High	High
Durability	High	Moderate	High
Established History	High	Moderate	Low
Divisability	Moderate	Moderate	High
Censorship Resistance	Moderate	Moderate	High
Verifiability	Moderate	Moderate	High
Scarcity	Moderate	Low	High
Smart/Programmable	Low	Moderate	High

Figure 4.10

- **Divisibility and Fungibility:** One bitcoin is made up of 100 million satoshis which can be divided into an additional thousand units on the Lightning Network as "millisats."
  There will only ever be 21 million bitcoin
  1 bitcoin = 100,000,000 satoshis
  1 satoshi = 1,000 millisats

  This makes bitcoin highly divisible against gold or fiat currencies. Bitcoin is also fungible, meaning it is interchangeable in terms of value. One bitcoin always equals another bitcoin, and one satoshi equals another satoshi.

- **Portability and Salability:** Bitcoin can be transmitted instantly worldwide. Its open network allows anyone to send and receive bitcoin as well as mine or run a node. For those wanting to transport bitcoin across borders without fear of theft, it is possible to carry it literally in their minds by memorizing 12 words that allow access to their bitcoin.

- **Scarcity:** Bitcoin has a hard cap of 21 million coins encoded into the source code. This is enforced by the hundreds of thousands of users running nodes all over the world running Bitcoin's source code (Bitcoin Core). No one can create more bitcoin.

- **Censorship Resistance:** Bitcoin is protected by its incentive and governance model. Bitcoin is a global network with millions of node operators and miners. If one miner decides not to include a specific transaction for whatever reason, another miner will pick it up, add it to a block, and get paid to do so. Censoring Bitcoin for personal gains contradicts economic incentives and actually results in financial loss.

- **Immutability and Verifiability:** Hundreds of thousands of nodes all over the globe are verifying that transactions are valid. Running a node is accessible to anyone with basic hardware, such as an old laptop. Due to ever-advancing technology, today you can run a node for less than $200, making it accessible to the majority of the world. Soon it may be possible for anyone to run a full node on their phones.

Security

Miners secure the network by finding new blocks and adding to the ledger. They do this by expending enormous amounts of energy to find blocks, adding transactions to those blocks, and receiving bitcoin from both the block subsidy and transaction fees. Think of this as Bitcoin's security system, similar to a massive armored truck convoy to transport gold or armed guards protecting vaults. Someone would need to control more than 50% of all the hashrate in order to even attempt an attack. This security framework makes the Bitcoin network virtually unhackable. How many times have you heard about bank data breaches in the last decade? How many times has your data been leaked? According to a survey done at Duke University, more than 80% of companies in the U.S. have been hacked.[69] Data from a University of Maryland study suggests there is one cyberattack every 39 seconds, or 2,200 per day.[70] Other data suggests it's double that number. The energy expended to provide Bitcoin's "proof of work," makes it virtually unhackable unless one expends more energy and deploys more miners than 50% of the network.

Today, bitcoin serves as a store of value across the globe. Anyone can store their time in this perfectly scarce, permissionless system.

This graph displays the price of bitcoin in U.S. dollars from 2015-2024 on a logarithmic scale:

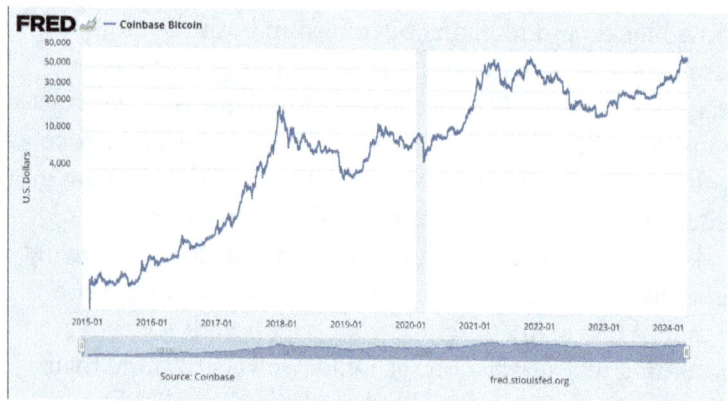

Figure 4.11 Source: Federal Bank of St. Louis[71]

This graph displays the purchasing power of the U.S. dollar from 2015-2024 on a logarithmic scale:

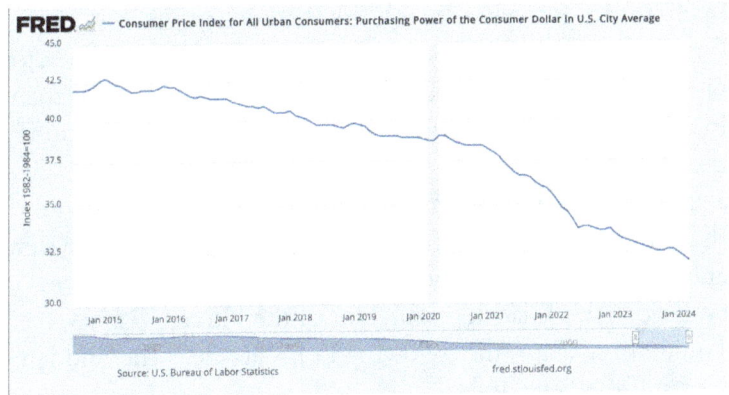

Figure 4.12 Source: Federal Bank of St. Louis[72]

FUD #4:
Bitcoin has no intrinsic value.

The process of assigning value to objects is fundamentally subjective. We, as humans, use money to quantify and rank the things we value. The concept of "intrinsic value" implies objects possess value independent of human perception, as if an object could be valuable to a person even if they do not recognize its worth. This notion is illogical. Ultimately, it is human judgment that assigns value.

If someone says, "Ok, but Bitcoin is not backed by anything." To address this particular piece of FUD, let's start with the dollar. The dollar is "backed," or rather, enforced, by the strength and influence of the U.S. military, along with the war, violence, bloodshed, and destruction that have been pivotal in establishing the U.S. and its currency in their present forms. Since the Bretton Woods Agreement post-World War II, the U.S. has maintained its status as the global reserve currency and has promoted the dollar worldwide in many forms, notably through the Petrodollar system. Originating in 1971, this system forced Saudi Arabia to price oil in dollars and stockpile U.S. debt. This of course led to an increase in demand for the dollar and solidified its position in the global economy. The U.S. government takes action against nations that attempt to conduct oil transactions in their own currencies, as this challenges the petrodollar system and the dominance of the U.S. dollar as the global reserve currency. Alex Gladstein, director of the Human Rights Foundation, states the following in his article, "The Hidden Costs of the Petrodollar,"

> By 1971, U.S. debt had simply grown too high. Just $11 billion in gold backed $24 billion in dollars. That August, French President Pompidou sent a battleship to New York City to collect his nation's gold holdings from the Federal Reserve, and the British asked the U.S. to prepare $3 billion worth of gold held in Fort Knox for withdrawal. In a televised speech on August 15, 1971, President Richard Nixon told the American people that the U.S. would no longer redeem dollars for gold as part of a plan that included wage and price freezes and an import surcharge in an attempt to save the economy. Nixon said closing the gold window was temporary, but few things are as permanent as temporary measures. As a result, the dollar was devalued by more than 10%, and the Bretton Woods system ceased to exist. The world entered a major financial crisis, though when asked about the impact that the "Nixon Shock" would have

on foreign nations, Nixon made his position clear: "I don't give a shit about the lira."[73]

That's not a system I want "backing" or "enforcing" my money. But does money actually need to be backed by anything? Does it need to have a "utility" value? A money's utility can contribute to its adoption, for instance, salt, tobacco, and gold have all been monies in the past. However, this utility becomes unnecessary once the item is established as money.

For instance, if gold were to lose all its industrial or "utility" uses (such as in electronics), while retaining its monetary qualities (being scarce and durable), its status and effectiveness as money would remain unchanged. So, why does Bitcoin need utility or "backing" beyond simply being money? It doesn't. If anything, one can argue Bitcoin is "backed" or "enforced" on a global scale by over 600 exahashes of mining power performing proof of work, hundreds of thousands of nodes running Bitcoin software, and its vast user base. Bitcoin is backed by its network. Bitcoin is backed by code. Bitcoin is backed by math. Bitcoin is backed by *energy*.

In December 1921, *The New York Tribune* published a story about Henry Ford's vision for the future of money titled "Ford Would Replace Gold With Energy Currency and Stop Wars." In it Ford states:

> Under the energy currency system the standard would be a certain amount of energy exerted for one hour that would be equal to one dollar. It's simply a case of thinking and calculating in terms different from those laid down to us by the international banking group to

which we have grown so accustomed that we think there is no other desirable standard.[74]

Ford predicted a money "backed" by energy over 100 years ago.

Unit of Account and Medium of Exchange

Bitcoin is an excellent store of value compared to all other forms of money and has increased in purchasing power since its inception. Many Bitcoiners are already using bitcoin as a unit of account. For example, I measure everything in bitcoin. My thinking goes, "1 million satoshis will be worth a lot more four years from now. Whereas four years ago, that same amount of satoshis could only buy a quarter of what they can buy today. That house I want? It will be cheaper in a few years when priced in bitcoin."

The very first bitcoin transaction was for 2 Papa John's pizzas in 2010. They cost 10,000 bitcoin. Those 10,000 bitcoin are worth well over $600 million today. Your average pizza today costs $25. That bitcoin could now buy over 24 million pizzas.

Life gets cheaper over time under a Bitcoin standard. Once you're in Bitcoin long enough and gain a deep understanding, you will start to automatically measure everything in bitcoin. You'll start to "think" in bitcoin as you see your fiat currency's purchasing power melt in your hand.

As adoption increases, bitcoin will be used more frequently as a medium of exchange, becoming a preferred method for transacting goods and services. As fiat currencies print themselves into collapse, I believe the world will gradually switch to a Bitcoin standard.

Money 101

"Bitcoin has no top, because the dollar has no bottom."

-Max Keiser

Bitcoin is already being used as a medium of exchange for goods and services and is facilitating seamless cross-border payments. The growth of the Lightning Network in recent years has been exponential, with the value transmitted over the network increasing and hundreds of Lightning companies emerging.

This is data from one of those companies, River, a Bitcoin exchange that runs a Lightning node:

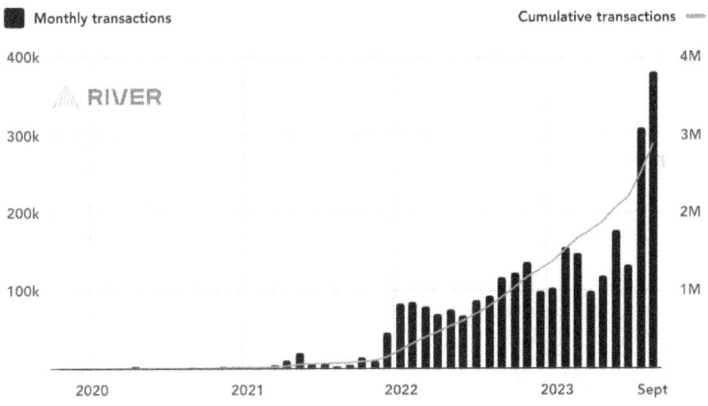

Figure 4.13 Source: River Research Report October 2023[75]

FUD #5:
Isn't there a better coin?

Over 99% of the other cryptocurrency coins are centrally controlled, meaning founders control and can modify any attribute of their coin over time. Many "crypto" projects were initial coin offering (ICO) Ponzi schemes that served as pump-and-dump strategies for their founders. By leveraging marketing tactics, their social media status, and hiring influencers, they generate hype and "pump up" the value of a coin, creating the exit liquidity needed to "dump" their coins on the market and make some fast cash.[76,77] Then, rinse and repeat. This cycle has been ongoing since 2017.

There are a few coins that are hard forks of Bitcoin, using parts of its original code, where one could argue no one actually controls them. However, they lack significant network effects. Very few people are actually contributing to these networks in the form of hashrate or running nodes. With minimal resources, one could dominate these networks, making them vulnerable to attacks. This is because these coins are missing some important properties of Bitcoin. For example, some have increased block sizes, leading to bloated blockchains that require huge hard drive space. This make running a node unaffordable for most, compromising decentralization and security. Some do not have a fixed supply cap (like Bitcoin's 21 million) allowing for endless issuance (inflation and devaluation), and while many claim to offer faster, cheaper transactions, innovations like the Lightning Network on Bitcoin have rendered such claims insignificant.

These alternative projects mirror the flaws of the current fiat system rather than presenting genuine innovation. Bitcoin is the only one that stands out as the true breakthrough, tackling and fixing all the problems at once, in a single system.

Bitcoin did not appear out of thin air. It was carefully crafted using 50 years of cryptographic history to address all the systemic issues with both digital and traditional money.

Everything that makes Bitcoin work:

- The supply cap of 21 million coins
- The coin issuance schedule—the block subsidy gets smaller over time causing deflation rather than inflation in a process called "The Halving."
- The difficulty adjustment—ensuring blocks are found at a 10-minute average, regardless of hashrate. As hashrate goes up, the difficulty in finding the correct number also goes up. If hashrate goes down, the difficulty gets easier.
- The block size limit to ensure easy and affordable node participation
- Proof of work mining and network consensus

These all contribute to making Bitcoin a groundbreaking achievement.

Satoshi Nakamoto ingeniously found a way to piece everything together to make a perfect form of money. The best part was that he disappeared soon after the launch of Bitcoin never to be heard from again. He, she, or they knew staying anonymous and disappearing were crucial for Bitcoin's survival as a decentralized currency without a central authority. The growth and distribution of coins could then happen organically by providing work to the network. To obtain bitcoin, one had to invest in the energy and ASICs to mine it, or had to spend money (time) to purchase it from others. This stands in contrast to many "crypto" projects that mint and distribute tokens out of thin air to their founders, without requiring any kind of work. This is similar to governments that print fiat currency at will, with no actual work or value creation involved to justify its issuance. Ultimately, both "crypto" projects and fiat currencies lead to an inflated money supply. Those positioned closest to the money spigot—whether founders or governments—reap the most benefits, at the expense of devaluing the currency for everyone else, in essence, stealing their time. Bitcoin's proof of work, supply cap, and decentralization solves this.

Any valuable features developed by other coins could be integrated into Bitcoin's higher layers, ensuring its base layer remains unaltered and secure. For instance, the Lightning Network acts as a second layer, enabling the development of third-layer applications without compromising Bitcoin's base layer security. This approach mirrors the structure of the internet and our monetary system, which emphasize scalability through layers rather than overloading a single blockchain with all functions—a common mistake in many "crypto" projects.

Bitcoin is the innovation. Bitcoin fixes money.

Unit bias is a cognitive bias where individuals tend to prefer a whole unit of something over a fractional part. If someone doesn't understand the fundamental properties and value of Bitcoin compared to other coins, they might say, "Why would I spend $70,000 on 1 bitcoin when I can buy 1000 of xyz coin for a penny each?" They judge the value based on its price per unit rather than its market value, often overlooking important factors such as total supply, market capitalization, and all properties that make Bitcoin unique.

This leads them to believe they're "late" to Bitcoin and need to invest in the next big opportunity. A way around this thinking is to denominate bitcoin in satoshis. "I can buy 1500 satoshis for $1."

FUD #6:
Only criminals use Bitcoin.

Fun fact: Roughly 90% of the dollar bills in circulation in the U.S. have been shown to contain cocaine residue.[78]

The United Nations Office on Drugs and Crime estimates as much as $2 trillion is illegally laundered around the world each year, or 5% of the total global money supply, with more than 90% of money laundering going undetected.[79,80]

In 2020, global banks were fined $10.4 billion for money laundering violations. Capital One topped the list of U.S. banks with a penalty of $390 million for neglecting to report a vast number of suspicious transactions.[81]

In 2023, only 1% of Bitcoin and all other cryptocurrencies combined, or around $22 billion, was sent from illicit addresses.[82] This suggests criminals prefer using the traditional banking system for their illegal operations.

Why is Bitcoin different? Bitcoin is a public ledger. Every transaction is recorded on the blockchain for everyone to see. This transparency fosters a system of accountability, holding individuals, financial institutions, and governments to a higher standard of honesty. Anyone can publish their address for the public to audit. For instance, the President of El Salvador, Nayib Bukele, published the country's bitcoin treasury reserve address to his X.com account for the public to monitor and audit.[83] Anyone can see the activity and balance of El Salvador's bitcoin holdings. This transparency marks a significant shift from the traditional practice of relying on financial institutions to accurately report their assets without manipulating the figures. Once public, anyone can track payments out of the address to their destinations.

Anyone can be fully transparent and auditable with Bitcoin. The Bitcoin ledger is public, yet the details of who is transacting and where transactions are directed remain confidential unless end users make their main wallet address public. Additionally, users and wallets can generate new addresses for each transaction to ensure privacy. The level of transparency depends on the user's privacy preferences. This specifically applies to transactions on the Bitcoin main chain. Payments made on the Lightning Network are even more private. Looking ahead, larger transactions, such as those by banks or exchanges consolidating daily activities, or governments adding to or spending from treasuries, or if someone is purchasing a car or buying a house, are likely to occur on the main chain. The Lightning Network is better suited and more cost-effective for smaller, everyday payments, which remain invisible to the public.

In contrast, the current financial system is a closed system, obscuring monetary transactions from public view. No one can be verifiably transparent, even if they wanted to be. This concealment potentially makes it easier for illicit collaborations between criminals and bankers in money laundering schemes.

Moreover, Bitcoin is a tool—a form of technology. A technology is not inherently good or bad; it depends on how it's used. For instance, criminals use cell phones. Should all cell phones be banned? Criminals use the internet. Should the internet be banned? And cars—they're used by criminals to get around. Should cars be banned? Of course not. The issue lies in the criminal actions, not the tools they happen to use.

FUD #7:
The government will ban Bitcoin.

Many countries have tried to ban Bitcoin and failed. China has tried to ban Bitcoin on three different occasions.[84] It always comes back stronger. The global and decentralized nature of Bitcoin's open source code makes it practically impossible to implement a geographical ban. If a government tries to outlaw Bitcoin, citizens will flee to friendlier jurisdictions. By banning Bitcoin, a jurisdiction not only forfeits its potential monetary benefits but also the second order benefits (such as energy production, infrastructure, and grid balancing). The result is a loss of both capital and citizens—a brain drain.

The China mining ban in May 2021 caused many miners to relocate to other jurisdictions such as the U.S. and Kazakhstan. Reports of several underground mining operations in China emerged shortly after the ban, and by September 2021, China had regained 22% of the total Bitcoin hashrate.[85]

Six months after the ban, the hashrate had fully recovered.

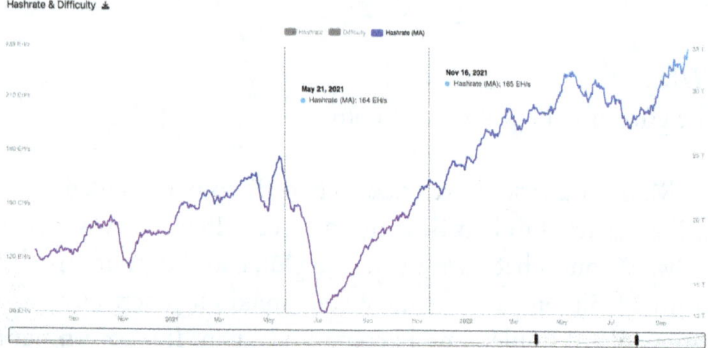

Figure 4.14 Source: mempool.space[86]

Nation State Adoption

El Salvador became the first country to adopt Bitcoin as legal tender in 2021. Following this move, the country has experienced significant growth in GDP, an increase in their credit ratings in 2023 (while the U.S. credit rating declined), and a substantial boost in tourism. [87] Previously solely dependent on the U.S. dollar as their currency and lacking any means to control or benefit from the money printing, El Salvador found a new path forward. The president's initial bill proposal for making Bitcoin legal tender stated, "In order to mitigate the negative impact from central banks, it becomes necessary to authorize the circulation of a digital currency with a supply that cannot be controlled by any central bank and is only altered in accord with objective and calculable criteria."[88]

El Salvador's journey and progression will be an intriguing case study on the future of money.

Adopting a new monetary system does take time. As fiat currencies continue to inflate and die out, volatility is inevitable. Positioning yourself with the harder, superior currency is crucial in retaining your wealth, your time, on the other side of an inflationary monetary system.

> "Humans have never been able to truly own anything before bitcoin, because everything else is either centralized or confiscatable, or both."
>
> -Unknown

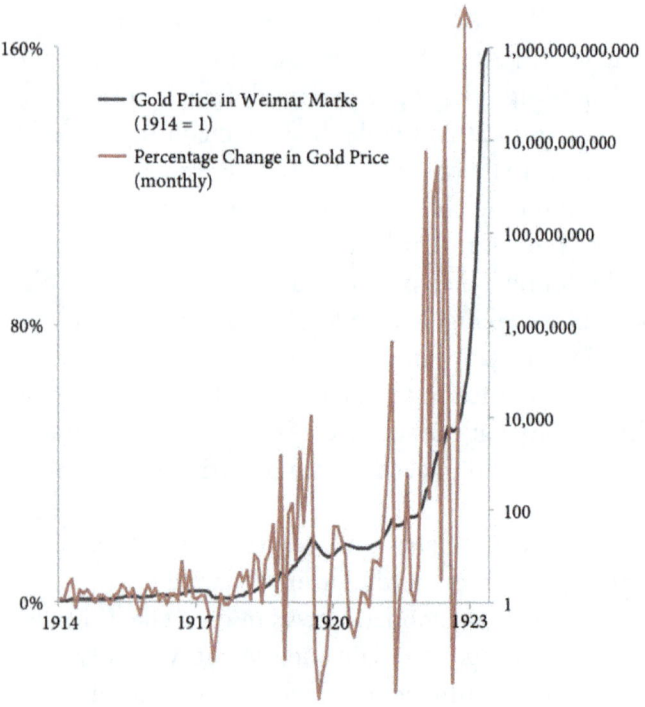

Figure 4.15 Source: @DylanLeclair, X.com[89]

This chart depicts the volatility and exponential trajectory of a hyperinflationary event in the Weimar Republic in Germany, tracking the local fiat currency, Weimar Marks, against gold from 1914-1923. Gold, the harder currency, shows extreme volatility until the mark's inevitable collapse. Zooming out, it's hard to see these violent up and down swings, just the mark being devalued slowly, then suddenly collapsing. This hyperinflationary spiral was triggered by

Money 101

Germany's excessive money printing in an attempt to meet the demands of World War I reparations.

Fortunately, now we have an escape hatch: Bitcoin.

Bitcoin is a system of <u>rules</u>, <u>not rulers</u>.

Bitcoin *fixes* remittance and cross border payments.
Bitcoin *fixes* inflation.
Bitcoin *fixes* storing one's time.
Bitcoin *fixes* the corrupt fiat system.
Bitcoin *fixes* money.

Part 3
The Future:
The Return of Sound Money

There are only two absolute scarce things in this world:
bitcoin and time.

What would returning to a sound money system look like? What if you didn't have to work your entire life at a job you dislike just to scrape by? What if you could work hard, live below your means, and save for 10 years to be free of financial restraints and pursue your passions? What if we could create lasting legacies, building things that could be handed down through generations? What if we could lift people out of extreme poverty by providing abundant energy, internet access, and fair money? Let's take a glimpse into a potential future.

Chapter 5

Lessons

"Our passion for learning ... is our tool for survival."

-Carl Sagan

Nihilism, the belief life is meaningless with no reason to hope for a better future, is a perspective increasingly common among young people today.[90,91] They feel a sense of despair and detachment, doubting the world can improve from what it is now. They often do not make plans, set goals, or strive to build anything meaningful; instead, they drift through life without purpose. With a future that's becoming increasingly expensive, no matter how hard they work, they find nothing seems to be within their reach, leading many to simply give up. This generation has come to realize their money holds little value tomorrow, driving them to indulge in immediate gratification today.[92,93] In China, frustrated youth have embraced the "Bai Lan" culture, which means "let it rot." This attitude reflects their refusal to put effort into anything because they see no purpose in doing so, leading them to give up on any aspirations.[94] A future without hope can trap individuals in a state of perpetual despair.

Lessons

The following are some of the changes I've noticed in myself since going down the Bitcoin rabbit hole:

Saving and Personal Accountability

Before diving into Bitcoin, I considered myself a fairly responsible person and competent at managing money. Looking back, it's honestly incredible how much money I threw away and the numerous opportunities I missed to secure my financial future. I lacked the laser-focus I have today.

Bitcoin has been instrumental in teaching me the value of saving. I consistently find ways to work smarter, maximizing my income while lowering expenses. I convert every leftover dollar into bitcoin. I know every satoshi I save puts me closer to my future goals. Seeing the compounding growth of my savings and purchasing power in bitcoin has been eye-opening.

Every bitcoin I own is one of the finite 21 million in existence, while every dollar I own is one of an infinite supply. Bitcoin is a deflationary currency that allows my purchasing power to grow over time. I would rather own a piece of a finite money supply that has superior properties than a piece of an infinite money supply with poor qualities that diminishes my purchasing power over time.

Now, I evaluate every non-essential purchase to determine if it's worth sacrificing my future purchasing power by spending it today instead of storing it in bitcoin. "I could buy this latte for $7, or I could buy $7 worth of sats." "I could buy a new car, or could I make do with my old one and put the difference into bitcoin." "I could buy an expensive house, or I could choose to rent, live below my means, and buy bitcoin with the savings." Because of this change in perception, bitcoin has greatly curbed my consumption habits.

The ability to become self-sovereign and custody my bitcoin without relying on a third party is a profound revelation. It belongs solely to me. I control the keys and am directly responsible for their safekeeping. I have the freedom to store and transmit value, regardless of where I live or my status in the world. No one can make more, control it, disable it, or destroy it—not even a government collapse. I can take and send my bitcoin anywhere in the world. I can access my bitcoin from any computer or smartphone anywhere in the world. I can memorize 12 words and carry my bitcoin in my head. It's a perfectly engineered money, unlike anything that came before it. How fortunate are we to witness this remarkable transformation in human history?

Time Preference

Bitcoin has lowered my time preference. I now think in terms of years, decades, and centuries, instead of minutes, hours, and days. I think, "What changes can I make now to improve my future? What changes can I make now that will help my 80-year-old self and the world she lives in?"

Bitcoin's influence on me has extended beyond finances. It encourages me to think about the wider aspects in my life and offers a sense of hope and optimism for the future. Motivated by this, I now invest in my future by eating healthier, exercising, engaging in activities that positively impact the planet, educating people about Bitcoin, and saving in bitcoin. By dedicating time and effort to these practices, I can help secure a better world for my 80-year-old self, while also ensuring she's around to enjoy it. I'm now building for the future.

Bitcoin has given back my time. I can now save the fruits of my labor in a finite, perfectly engineered money that will preserve my time throughout my life. It's given me a future. It's given me freedom. Before Bitcoin, if I didn't spend my money relatively quickly, that time would begin to disappear. My 80-year-old self will appreciate that time. My 50-year-old self will appreciate that time.

Chapter 6

Hope for the Future

"It might make sense just to get some in case it catches on."

-Satoshi Nakamoto on Bitcoin in 2009

A Deflationary World

It's Friday night in 2004, and you just snagged the latest DVD release at Blockbuster. You wait in line, hand the cashier your money, verify you don't have any overdue charges, and then…freedom! You drive home, and pop that baby in the DVD player. What a time to be alive.

How much the world has changed.

Our media became digitized. Smartphones dominated, app stores emerged, streaming movies became the norm. Our books, music, movies, and shows all transitioned to digital formats, accessible from any smart device. Accessing media became instant, and the costs to access it dropped. You could now pay $15/month for a Netflix subscription and watch thousands of movies without ever leaving your home.

You no longer have the cost of making a DVD, packaging it, shipping it to a retail location, or the cost of operating that store. Additionally, the time and travel costs associated with going to the store to rent that DVD, as well as the return journey, no longer exist.

Hope for the Future

Technology increases productivity. Productivity naturally causes prices to fall. Books that once filled a grand library can now fit on an iPad. You no longer have to print, bind, or store warehouses full of physical books. Physical tools like compasses or calculators can now be replaced by free apps on your phone.

This price savings technology brings should be fully passed on to humanity. Yet, the inflationary nature of our monetary system is at odds with this deflationary trend. As productivity increases, prices should decrease, reducing the need for people to work as hard or as often as they once did. Life should be getting cheaper and easier.

Yet, people are struggling. They're working two or three jobs and just barely scraping by. They're running on a hamster wheel that seems to be spinning faster and faster. No matter how hard they work, life just seems to be getting more expensive.

Bitcoin emerges as a beacon of hope in this scenario, offering a deflationary money for the deflationary world that technology brings. If we saved the fruits of our labor in bitcoin, our money would more accurately mirror our advancements in productivity, enhancing purchasing power and the overall quality of life technology brings.

Shouldn't we have a money that aligns with the natural deflationary trends of technological progress? And shouldn't our money be digital in this new digitized age, offering access anytime and from anywhere, enabling instant, borderless transactions? Why do we need to rely on intermediaries such as governments and banks to be our "blockbusters?" Why do they control the supply of money? Bitcoin cuts out the middlemen. Bitcoin is a technology that increases productivity and puts the power and control back in the hands of the user.

> "Lost coins only make everyone else's coins worth slightly more. Think of it as a donation to everyone."
>
> - Satoshi Nakamoto

A Peaceful World

For most of my life, the United States has been at war. To fund these conflicts, the government has ramped up money printing, both domestically and abroad. This printing not only increases inflation, but devalues the government's debts, as the erosion of purchasing power makes these debts worth less over time. As purchasing power decreases, so do government debts, creating an endless cycle of financing wars through money printing and debt devaluation.

In the past, the government would issue war bonds to raise funds, relying on the voluntary financial support of its citizens. Now, it's easier to just print money and bypass the citizens directly. This slowly robs the citizens of their purchasing power over time without many of them noticing or realizing why their money is worth less.

Adopting a currency that cannot be printed out of thin air might disincentivize future war. Without the ability to print more money, funding a war becomes challenging. It would require the consent of the citizens to allocate their money, their stored time, to go to war.

Eliminating access to the money printer could reduce government corruption around the world. Both governments and individuals would be bound to the same rules as everyone else. Bitcoin levels the playing field by enforcing the same rules on all participants, without any unfair advantages. With Bitcoin, you commit to a system where spending beyond your means results in a direct personal loss of wealth. There are no bailouts. There is no money printer that's going to save you. This creates an environment where everyone is responsible for their own decisions and actions. It's a fair playing field—a system of rules, not rulers.

A Prosperous World

During the Renaissance in Europe, an era thriving under the gold standard, society embraced a philosophy of building things to last. Artists painstakingly created marble sculptures and works of art that took decades, masterpieces we can still enjoy today. Beautiful buildings were constructed out of solid stone that have stood the test of time. People had a lower time preference and meticulously planned these projects to ensure their work could be appreciated by future generations.

Perhaps Bitcoin can return us to a time of building things that last. Many things in today's society are built for functional obsolescence rather than longevity, quality, and repairability. With the stability of having sound money, we have the freedom to step away from the daily grind and pursue our passions. We can finally step off that hamster wheel. We can lower our time preference, investing time and efforts into our projects with patience and foresight, ensuring what we build not only lasts but also enhances the lives of both ourselves and future generations.

Bitcoin also has the potential to foster an age of energy abundance, lifting people out of extreme poverty, expanding internet access, and extending lifespans. Bitcoin monetizes the building of electrical grid infrastructure and renewable resources, reducing our reliance on fossil fuels.

The energy abundance alone can return us to a period of building things that last. If anything, Bitcoin can help to secure more reliable infrastructure and a more abundant and environmentally sustainable future for our planet.

Game Theory

As society advances, embracing new technology becomes not just helpful but crucial for our survival and success. The message throughout history has been clear: embrace technology or get left behind. Historical transitions, such as the shift from traditional bows to firearms, from candlelight to electricity, from horses to cars, from traditional mail to email, and from landlines to cell phones, illustrate the inevitable trajectory toward more efficient and capable technologies.

Daily Mail, December 5, 2000:

Figure 6.1 Source: Daily Mail[95]

The internet represents a huge leap in this progression, bringing endless opportunities for knowledge, connectivity, and economic growth. Those who resist or delay embracing these advancements not only jeopardize their own success but also risk being sidelined in a rapidly advancing world. It's not about discarding the old for the sake of the new; it's about embracing technologies that unlock incredible possibilities for progress and well-being. The choice is clear: adapt or risk being left behind.

In today's world, adopting Bitcoin provides individuals and nations with substantial advantages over traditional monetary systems. Early adopters of this technology will disproportionately benefit compared to those who are last, similar to the advantage early adopters of firearms gained over those who clung to arrows. By embracing Bitcoin early, you can exchange your depreciating fiat currencies for a superior form of money that appreciates over time. Bitcoin not only increases your purchasing power, but also allows you to enjoy all the direct and indirect benefits discussed throughout this book.

Fighting against new technologies has always been a losing strategy. At least from a financial standpoint, it's in one's best interest to participate in new networks and technologies rather than attack them. Game theory suggests participating in the Bitcoin network aligns with humanity's best interests, guiding us toward a more fair and prosperous world.

Bitcoin is Hope.

Final Thoughts

Bitcoin encompasses a diverse range of fields, including history, economics, game theory, computer science, psychology, energy, math, physics, networks, geopolitics, human rights, sociology, and finance. I've learned more studying Bitcoin over the last four years than I've learned in all my years of schooling combined. I encourage you to dive deeper into Bitcoin and follow the Bitcoin ethos: "Don't trust, verify." As you embark on your Bitcoin journey, I hope this book has provided a solid foundation and sparked your curiosity to explore further.

I bid you well on your travels down the Bitcoin rabbit hole.

Continue down the rabbit hole:
BitcoinLearn.org

Endnotes

All websites were accessed in April 2024.

[1] "Money Transfer Fees." *Western Union*. Last modified March 11, 2021. https://www.westernunion.com/blog/en/us-money-transfer-fees/.

[2] "Price Estimator," *Western Union*. https://www.westernunion.com/us/en/send-money/app/price-estimator/.

[3] Strike. https://strike.me.

[4] "Western Union (WU) - Revenue." *Companies Market Cap*. https://companiesmarketcap.com/western-union/revenue/.

[5] A Web Analysis, "Convert Satoshi to USD Dollar and USD to Satoshi." https://awebanalysis.com/en/convert-satoshi-to-dollar-usd/.

[6] "Bitcoin Network Hashrate Hits All-Time High After China Crypto Ban." *CNBC*. Last modified December 10, 2021. https://www.cnbc.com/2021/12/10/bitcoin-network-hashrate-hits-all-time-high-after-china-crypto-ban.html#:~:text=But%20after%20Beijing%20effectively%20banished,about%20113%25%20in%20five%20months.

[7] Carter, N. "Go West, Bitcoin: Unpacking the Great Hashrate Migration." *CoinDesk*. June 22, 2021. https://www.coindesk.com/policy/2021/06/22/go-west-bitcoin-unpacking-the-great-hashrate-migration/.

[8] "Mining Hashrate and Difficulty Graphs." *Mempool.Space*. https://mempool.space/graphs/mining/hashrate-difficulty#all.

9 "Climate Warming Likely to Cause Large Increases in Wetland Methane Emissions." *U.S. Geological Survey.* March 2, 2023. https://www.usgs.gov/news/featured-story/climate-warming-likely-cause-large-increases-wetland-methane-emissions .

10 "Abandoned Oil & Gas Wells." *SciLine.* November 30, 2023. https://www.sciline.org/environment-energy/abandoned-oil-gas-wells/.

11 Goldstein, J. "New Study Confirms Flaring is a Nationwide Problem Requiring Urgent Action." Environmental Defense Fund. September 30, 2022. https://blogs.edf.org/energyexchange/2022/09/30/new-study-confirms-flaring-is-a-nationwide-problem-requiring-urgent-action/ .

12 "Inefficient and unlit natural gas flares both emit large quantities of methane." *Science.* September 29, 2022. https://www.science.org/doi/10.1126/science.abq0385 .

13 "Vehicle Ownership in Los Angeles County." *Los Angeles Almanac.* https://www.laalmanac.com/transport/tr02.php.

14 MIT Climate Portal Writing Team. "How Much Does Natural Gas Contribute to Climate Change Through CO2 Emissions When the Fuel is Burned?" *MIT Climate Portal.* July 17, 2023. https://climate.mit.edu/ask-mit/how-much-does-natural-gas-contribute-climate-change-through-co2-emissions-when-fuel-burned .

15 "Car Ownership Statistics." *MoneyGeek.* Last updated March 1, 2024. https://www.moneygeek.com/insurance/auto/car-ownership-statistics/.

16 "Basic Information about Landfill Gas." *U.S. Environmental Protection Agency.* Last updated March 22, 2024. https://www.epa.gov/lmop/basic-information-about-landfill-gas.

[17] Volcovici, V. "Aerial Surveys Show US Landfills are Major Source of Methane Emissions." Reuters. March 28, 2024. https://www.reuters.com/world/us/aerial-surveys-show-us-landfills-are-major-source-methane-emissions-2024-03-28/.

[18] "Landfill Methane Regulations Workshop." *California Air Resources Board*. May 18, 2023. https://ww2.arb.ca.gov/sites/default/files/2023-05/LMR-workshop_05-18-2023.pdf.

[19] Mellerud, J., & Helseth, A. "Bitcoin Mining Using Stranded Natural Gas is the Most Cost-Effective Way to Reduce Emissions." K33.com. September 5, 2022. https://k33.com/research/archive/articles/bitcoin-mining-using-stranded-natural-gas-is-the-most-cost-effective-way-to.

[20] Dergigi. "How Bitcoin Mining Can Transform the Energy Industry." September 3, 2022. https://dergigi.com/assets/files/2022-09-03-arcane-research-how-bitcoin-mining-can-transform-the-energy-industry.pdf.

[21] Hengevoss, D. "Waste-to-energy options in municipal solid waste management. A guide for decision makers in developing and emerging countries." May 2017. https://www.researchgate.net/publication/317427399_Waste-to-energy_options_in_municipal_solid_waste_management_A_guide_for_decision_makers_in_developing_and_emerging_countries .

[22] "Crypto-Assets and Climate Report." *Executive Office of the President.* September 2022. Accessed at https://www.whitehouse.gov/wp-content/uploads/2022/09/09-2022-Crypto-Assets-and-Climate-Report.pdf .

[23] Gridless. "At the Frontier of Bitcoin Mining in Africa." Gridless Compute. Last updated 2024. https://gridlesscompute.com.

[24] "This chocolate factory is powered by a net-zero bitcoin mine." *World Economic Forum*. Last updated 2024. https://www.weforum.org/videos/bitcoin-mine-power/.

25 Jackson, R. B., Ahlström, A., Hugelius, G., Wang, C., Porporato, A., Ramaswami, A., Roy, J., & Yin, J. "Human well-being and per capita energy use." April 12, 2022. Ecosphere, 13(4), e3978. https://esajournals.onlinelibrary.wiley.com/doi/10.1002/ecs2.3978.

26 "Energy Use Per Person vs. GDP Per Capita." *Our World in Data*. 2021. https://ourworldindata.org/grapher/energy-use-per-person-vs-gdp-per-capita .

27 "Access to Electricity." *IAE*. https://www.iea.org/reports/sdg7-data-and-projections/access-to-electricity.

28 "2021 Texas Power Crisis." *Wikipedia*. https://en.wikipedia.org/wiki/2021_Texas_power_crisis.

29 Vu, K., & Foxhall, E. "Why Can't More Texans Profit Like Bitcoin Miners for Using Less Power?" *The Texas Tribune*. January 3, 2024. https://www.texastribune.org/2024/01/03/texas-bitcoin-profit-electricity/.

30 "Riot Showcases Demand Response Strategy: Bitcoin Mining's Role in Strengthening Texas Energy Grid." *Bitcoin News*. https://news.bitcoin.com/riot-showcases-demand-response-strategy-bitcoin-minings-role-in-strengthening-texas-energy-grid.

31 "Bitcoin Mining: Riot Uses 'Demand Response' Strategy in Texas and Receives $31.7 Million in Energy Credits." *Cryptonomist*. September 8, 2023. https://en.cryptonomist.ch/2023/09/08/bitcoin-mining-riot-demand-response-strategy/.

32 Level39 [@level39]. (2022, July 16). [Tweet]. Twitter. https://twitter.com/level39/status/1548550264218583040?lang=en.

[33] "Bitcoin Mining Council Survey Confirms Year on Year Improvements in Sustainable Power and Technological Efficiency in H1-2023." *Bitcoin Mining Council.* August 9, 2023. https://bitcoinminingcouncil.com/bitcoin-mining-council-survey-confirms-year-on-year-improvements-in-sustainable-power-and-technological-efficiency-in-h1-2023/.

[34] "Bitcoin Mining Council Survey: Improvements in Sustainable Power and Technological Efficiency in H1-2023." *Bitcoin Mining Council.* August 2023. https://bitcoinminingcouncil.com/wp-content/uploads/2023/08/BMC-H1-2023-Presentation.pdf.

[35] "These dirty power plants cost billions and only operate in summer. Can they be replaced?" *Grist.* May 8, 2020. https://grist.org/justice/these-dirty-power-plants-cost-billions-and-only-operate-in-summer-can-they-be-replaced/.

[36] HodlRev. [@HodlRev]. (2024, February 23). [Tweet]. Twitter. https://twitter.com/HodlRev/status/1760998502161666259.

[37] HodlRev. [@HodlRev]. (2023, July 19). [Tweet]. Twitter. https://twitter.com/HodlRev/status/1681835542109888512?ref_src=twsrc%5Etfw%7Ctwcamp%5Etweetembed%7Ctwterm%5E1681835542109888512%7Ctwgr%5E72f487916da4c4bbaf2f44d045c41c899f08b7fe%7Ctwcon%5Es1_&ref_url=https%3A%2F%2Fblockworks.co%2Fnews%2Fbitcoin-mining-drying-laundry.

[38] "Sustainable Bitcoin Miner Uses Waste Heat to Dry Wood." *CoinTelegraph.* https://cointelegraph.com/news/sustainable-bitcoin-miner-uses-waste-heat-to-dry-wood.

[39] "7 Wild Bitcoin Mining Rigs." *CoinDesk.* March 24, 2022. https://www.coindesk.com/layer2/2022/03/24/7-wild-bitcoin-mining-rigs.

[40] HodlRev. [@HodlRev]. (2023, April 10). [Tweet]. Twitter. https://twitter.com/HodlRev/status/1760998502161666259.

41 Ahmad, Z., & Conway, T. "Floodplain reclamation leads to loss of wetland ecosystem services." Ecosphere, 13(3), e03978. Ecological Society of America. 2022. https://esajournals.onlinelibrary.wiley.com/doi/10.1002/ecs2.3978.

42 Rybarczyk, R., Armstrong, D., & Fabiano, A. "On Bitcoin's Energy Consumption: A Quantitative Approach to a Subjective Question." *Galaxy Digital Mining.* May 2021. https://docsend.com/view/adwmdeeyfvqwecj2.

43 "Andreas Antonopoulos - 51% Bitcoin Attack." Video. Posted by "Rodolfo Díaz," YouTube. April 25, 2015. https://www.youtube.com/watch?v=ncPyMUfNyVM.

44 "ASIC Bitcoin Mining Hardware Market." *Business Research Insights.* April 1, 2024. https://www.businessresearchinsights.com/market-reports/asic-bitcoin-mining-hardware-market-109497.

45 Vivek. [@Vivek4real_]. (2024, April 6). [Tweet]. Twitter. https://x.com/Vivek4real_/status/1780911539127476547.

46 "The Time for Democracy Is Now." *Human Rights Foundation.* September 15, 2022. https://hrf.org/the-time-for-democracy-is-now/.

47 Gladstein, Alex. *Check Your Financial Privilege.* BTC Media, LLC, 2022, p. 4.

48 "Interactive Executive Summary Visualization." *World Bank.* 2021. https://www.worldbank.org/en/publication/globalfindex/interactive-executive-summary-visualization.

49 Gladstein, Alex. "Bitcoin Financial Freedom in Afghanistan." *Bitcoin Magazine.* Last modified August 23, 2021. https://bitcoinmagazine.com/culture/bitcoin-financial-freedom-in-afghanistan.

[50] "The Ultimate Bitcoin Use Cases with Alex Gladstein." Posted by *What Bitcoin Did*. YouTube. April 8, 2024. https://www.youtube.com/watch?v=TI3Xcei8d_I.

[51] "Remittances." *Migration Data Portal*. https://www.migrationdataportal.org/themes/remittances.

[52] "2012–2013 Cypriot Financial Crisis." *Wikipedia*. https://en.wikipedia.org/wiki/2012%E2%80%932013_Cypriot_financial_crisis.

[53] "Depositors in two Cypriot banks have lost a significant amount of money due to a banking crisis linked to the east Mediterranean island." *Reuters*. https://www.reuters.com/article/idUSKBN1K323Z/#:~:text=Depositors%20in%20two%20Cypriot%20banks,to%20the%20east%20Mediterranean%20island.

[54] Gladstein, Alex. *Check Your Financial Privilege*. BTC Media, LLC, 2022, p. 10.

[55] Gladstein, Alex. *Check Your Financial Privilege*. BTC Media, LLC, 2022, p. 4.

[56] "Consumer Price Index for All Urban Consumers: Rent of Primary Residence." *Federal Reserve Bank of St. Louis*. https://fred.stlouisfed.org/series/CUUR0000SA0R.

[57] "M2 Money Stock." *Federal Reserve Bank of St. Louis*. https://fred.stlouisfed.org/series/M2SL.

[58] "DataMapper: Inflation Rate, Average Consumer Prices." *International Monetary Fund*. https://www.imf.org/external/datamapper/PCPIPCH@WEO/WEOWORLD/VEN.

[59] "Lebanon's Fragile Economy Pulled Back into Recession." *World Bank*. https://www.worldbank.org/en/news/press-release/2023/12/21/lebanon-s-fragile-economy-pulled-back-into-recession.

60 KobeissiLetter. [@KobeissiLetter]. (2024, March 27). [Tweet]. Twitter. https://twitter.com/KobeissiLetter/status/1772962595126878402.

61 "Median Sales Price of Houses Sold for the United States." *Federal Reserve Bank of St. Louis.* https://fred.stlouisfed.org/series/MSPUS.

62 "NASDAQ Composite Index." *Federal Reserve Bank of St. Louis.* https://fred.stlouisfed.org/series/NASDAQCOM.

63 "Corporate Profits After Tax (without IVA and CCAdj)." *Federal Reserve Bank of St. Louis.* https://fred.stlouisfed.org/series/CP.

64 Driebusch, Corrie. "Red Ink Floods IPO Market." *Wall Street Journal.* October 1, 2018. https://www.wsj.com/articles/red-ink-floods-ipo-market-1538388000?utm_source=newsletter&utm_medium=email&utm_campaign=newsletter_axiosprorata&stream=top.

65 U.S. Debt Clock.org. (2024). https://www.usdebtclock.org/.

66 "A Peek Inside Fort Knox: The Most Heavily Guarded Military Base." MyBaseGuide. 2024. https://mybaseguide.com/inside-fort-knox.

67 "Series of 1928 (United States Currency)." *Wikipedia.* April 14, 2024. https://en.wikipedia.org/wiki/Series_of_1928_(United_States_Currency).

68 "Persistence of slave labor exposes lawlessness of Amazon gold mines." *Mongabay.* March 4, 2021. https://news.mongabay.com/2021/03/persistence-of-slave-labor-exposes-lawlessness-of-amazon-gold-mines/.

69 Duke Today Staff. "New CFO Survey: More Than 80 Percent of Firms Say They've Been Hacked." *Duke Today.* June 5, 2015. https://today.duke.edu/2015/06/cfohacking.

[70] "Hackers Attack Every 39 Seconds." *Security Magazine.* February 10, 2017. https://www.securitymagazine.com/articles/87787-hackers-attack-every-39-seconds.

[71] "Coinbase Bitcoin." *Federal Reserve Bank of St. Louis.* https://fred.stlouisfed.org/series/CBBTCUSD.

[72] "Consumer Price Index for All Urban Consumers: Purchasing Power of the Consumer Dollar in U.S. City Average (CUUR0000SA0R)." *Federal Reserve Bank of St. Louis.* https://fred.stlouisfed.org/series/CUUR0000SA0R.

[73] Gladstein, Alex. "UNCOVERING THE HIDDEN COSTS OF THE PETRODOLLAR: The world's reserve currency relies on oil, dictators, inequality and the military-industrial complex. But a Bitcoin standard could change this." *Bitcoin Magazine.* Original: April 28, 2021. Updated: September 21, 2021. https://bitcoinmagazine.com/culture/the-hidden-costs-of-the-petrodollar.

[74] "100 years ago, Henry Ford proposed 'energy currency' to replace gold." *Cointelegraph.* September 18, 2021. https://cointelegraph.com/news/100-years-ago-henry-ford-proposed-energy-currency-to-replace-gold.

[75] "The Lightning Network Grew by 1212% in 2 Years: Why It's Time to Pay Attention." *River Financial.* October 2023. https://river.com/learn/files/river-lightning-report-2023.pdf.

[76] Norlund, Chris. "How Social Media Influencers Fed Bankman-Fried's Cult of Personality." *CoinDesk.* January 18, 2023. https://www.coindesk.com/consensus-magazine/2023/01/18/how-social-media-influencers-fed-bankman-frieds-cult-of-personality/.

[77] Knight, Oliver. "US SEC Charges Kim Kardashian for Promoting EthereumMax." *CoinDesk.* Published October 3, 2022. Updated May 11, 2023. https://www.coindesk.com/business/2022/10/03/us-sec-charges-kim-kardashian-for-promoting-ethereummax/.

78 "Dickinson College Chemistry Class Explores the Presence of Drug Residue on U.S. Currency." *Dickinson College.* https://www.dickinson.edu/news/article/3193/dickinson_college_chemistry_class_explores_the_presence_of_drug_residue_on_us_currency#:~:text=Here's%20a%20startling%20fact%3A%20Roughly,shown%20to%20contain%20cocaine%20residue.

79 "Overview of Money Laundering." *United Nations Office on Drugs and Crime (UNODC).* https://www.unodc.org/unodc/en/money-laundering/overview.html.

80 Kolmar, Chris. "Money Laundering Statistics." *Zippia.* March 29, 2023. https://www.zippia.com/advice/money-laundering-statistics/.

81 "The War Against Money Laundering Is Being Lost." *The Economist.* April 12, 2021. https://www.economist.com/finance-and-economics/2021/04/12/the-war-against-money-laundering-is-being-lost.

82 "2024 Crypto Money Laundering." *Chainalysis.* https://www.chainalysis.com/blog/2024-crypto-money-laundering/.

83 Bukele, N. [@nayibbukele]. (2024, March 14). [Tweet]. X. https://x.com/nayibbukele/status/1768425845163503738.

84 Parker, Emily. (2024). "China Never Completely Banned Crypto." *CoinDesk.* Published February 5, 2024. Updated March 8, 2024. https://www.coindesk.com/consensus-magazine/2024/02/05/china-never-completely-banned-crypto/.

85 Browne, Ryan. "Bitcoin production roars back in China despite Beijing's ban on crypto mining." *CNBC.* May 18, 2022. https://www.cnbc.com/2022/05/18/china-is-second-biggest-bitcoin-mining-hub-as-miners-go-underground.html.

[86] "Graphs - Hashrate and Difficulty." *Mempool*. https://mempool.space/graphs/mining/hashrate-difficulty#all.

[87] "El Salvador Emerges as the Fastest-Growing Tourism Destination in Latin America." *El Salvador in English*. February 21, 2024. https://elsalvadorinenglish.com/2024/02/21/el-salvador-emerges-as-the-fastest-growing-tourism-destination-in-latin-america/.

[88] Bukele, N. [@nayibbukele]. (2021, June 5). [Tweet]. Twitter. https://twitter.com/nayibbukele/status/1401327906178191366.

[89] LeClair, D. (2021, May 24). [Tweet]. Twitter. https://x.com/dylanleclair_/status/1396518689177063429?s=46&t=ik35cjZcPlRTrbHDfsTz-w.

[90] Hess, Abigail Johnson. "51% of Young Americans Say They Feel Down, Depressed, or Hopeless." *CNBC*. May 10, 2021. https://www.cnbc.com/2021/05/10/51percent-of-young-americans-say-they-feel-down-depressed-or-hopeless.html.

[91] Webb, Charles Harper, Ph.D. "Increase in Nihilism Plays Havoc on Mental Health." *Psychology Today*. August 2022. https://www.psychologytoday.com/us/blog/drawing-the-curtains-back/202208/increase-in-nihilism-plays-havoc-mental-health.

[92] Mena, Bryan. "Young Americans Giving Up Owning a Home." *CNN*. February 3, 2024. https://www.cnn.com/2024/02/03/economy/young-americans-giving-up-owning-a-home/index.html.

[93] Strachan, Maxwell. "Teens Are Developing Severe Gambling Problems as Online Betting Surges." *Vice*. October 11, 2023. https://www.vice.com/en/article/4a37mp/teens-are-developing-severe-gambling-problems-as-online-betting-surges.

[94] "China youth reject hustle culture, face unemployment, economic uncertainty." *CNBC*. September 16, 2022. https://www.cnbc.com/2022/09/16/china-youth-reject-hustle-culture-face-unemployment-economic-uncertainty.html.

[95] Chapman, J. "Internet 'may be just a passing fad as millions give up on it.'" *Daily Mail*. December 5, 2000, p. 33.

www.ingramcontent.com/pod-product-compliance
Lightning Source LLC
Chambersburg PA
CBHW070148230526
45471CB00002B/577